"When I first got sober, I had a hard time with the God thing in AA. As far as I was concerned, the whole idea of God was great in theory, but in practice, a complete let-down. In the rooms, there was so much talk about God, I thought I could not do this simple program. Then some wise person pointed out to me that there was certainly a power greater than I (because if not, we're all fucked), but it didn't have to look like the God of my youth; it didn't even have to be called "God". What a relief. David Vartabedian has taken this understanding and elucidated it so that through his words, even the hardened, God-denying alcoholic can find her or his way to the most liberating condition available to human being: sobriety."

Brian O'Dea
Author, *High*, published by Random House Canada

"*Twelve Steps Without God* is a great alternative for accessing the source of power necessary for a psychic change necessary to overcome the disease of addiction. David's personal story and history of living the life of an active addict and his miraculous transformation will open the door for so many who are desperately seeking freedom from addiction. His many years of experience working in the field of recovery provide a powerful, effective, and long-lasting solution for long-term recovery."

Samantha Matern
Addictions Specialist and Counselor
Unityholisticlifecoach.com

Chris,

Thanks for all
your Love & support

TWELVE STEPS WITHOUT GOD

an energetic path to recovery

TWELVE STEPS WITHOUT GOD

an energetic path to recovery

David Vartabedian

enCompass

Published 2020 by enCompass Editions, Canada
© 2020 David Vartabedian
Printed in the U.S.A.
ISBN paperback edition 978-1-927664-15-5
ISBN clothbound edition 978-1-927664-16-2

encompass
EDITIONS

TABLE OF CONTENTS

Dedicated to the loving memory of my mother Doris Grace
and to
my beloved daughter Maya Grace Vartabedian

ACKNOWLEDGEMENTS

I'd like to express my love and gratitude for all the people, places and experiences that have helped me with this book.

First, thank you to all my friends, clients, people I've sponsored in recovery, and everyone who has sat through my classes and lectures—who just listened. And, to the client who first texted me that if I wrote this book, he believed that I would help a lot of people.

That encouraging text came to me one night as I was having dinner with Stephanie Culet. Stephanie has been there from the book's inception, she has read every chapter as I wrote it and has been so supportive and loving throughout. She helped me through the process more than she knows and has left an indelible mark on my life.

Thank you to Colin Broderick, who read the first draft, encouraged me to keep going and gave me productive guidance when it came to telling my most personal stories. Thank you, Josie Green, who read some of my first writings for the book, believed in it and me, and told me, "Do not hold back."

My thanks go also to Ashley Self, a dear friend and a brilliant editor who did the first manuscript edit; Megan Starks, who reviewed my work, adding stories and helping to get them published on www. thefix.com, the online magazine for the recovery community; and Celine Parris, who read drafts and inspired me to keep moving in the right direction.

Thank you to Sydney Walker, who read and reread drafts,and gave love and support as I went through the process of becoming a first-time author. Thank you, Samantha Matern, who sat with me, patiently telling me what flowed—and what didn't. Both Sydney and Samantha have been dear friends to me in my writing and sobriety: thank you.

My deepest gratitude goes to two writer friends who generously shared their experience and contacts with me: best-selling author Caroline Paul, who helped me connect with editors and agents, telling them, "I don't know if he can write, but he's very persistent;"and award-winning author Brian O'Dea, who graciously put me in touch with his writing network and gave me always sound advice.

Thank you to my daughter, Maya, who makes me proud to be her dad every day. She inspires me with her kindness, enthusiasm and creativity in living her life. I love you, Lolly bird.

Like raising a child, it takes a village to write a book—mine, anyway. Thank you to everyone who believed in me. My sister, Darity Wesley, provided me with direction, love and support not only with my book, but in my life. She is a spiritual guru. I also thank my mother, Doris Grace, who has been my inspiration throughout my life. She was not just my mom, she was a mentor in my recovery. Josh Brolin encouraged me to write, rewrite and read everything I could; he was so supportive and loving through the whole process, Thank you, my dear friend and brother.

A huge thank you to the writer Pam Janis, whose editing helped me take this book to the next level, first through long phone calls as we edited drafts from two coasts, and then working side-by-side in Washington, D.C., where we laughed as hard as we worked.

Thank you all so much for your love and support.

Finally, I'm so grateful to The Barn, my home, whose peace inspired me to write and created space for me to stay focused. It sits in one of the most beautiful places in California, the Hollister

Ranch on the Gaviota Coast, in the middle of an avocado orchard. With the Pacific Ocean at my front door, there was no better environment for me in which to write. It healed me and made it possible to share my journey in recovery with you who reads this.

FOREWORD

I don't know what a good book on sobriety is but I know that sobriety is good and I know that reading is good. And if the two can come together on a personal level and help one to achieve a less self-destructive and more spiritual life, then I'm all for it. This book was written by my friend David, who is achieving what all of us in insobriety attempt: recovery.

Recovery is a very personal thing, as is the God concept. We must feel on our own what that very powerful energy—that ultimately protective energy—means for each of us. This book for some may shed a light on that aspect of recovery, and as with everything in sobriety, take what works and discard the rest to use at some other milestone or junction in your recovery. But take what works and use it as if your life depended on it. I'm excited to comment on what has not only worked for him but for all the people he's impacted in the recovery community. David has helped thousands of people attain a life of contentment and relative peace. I'm very proud of my friend.

I hope this book gives you the elements that you may be looking for to further ensconce yourself in this way of life. David has affected me through his sobriety and my hope is that I may help spread his valuable experiences to you who may be looking for this perspective on what is to me the greatest gift we alcoholics have been given: a way to live freely without the insanity of a dehydrated spiritual life.

Sincerely,

Josh Brolin

PREFACE

In writing this book, I hope to inspire more people to take the opportunity to recover from their alcoholism or other addiction by applying the 12 Steps to their lives. My approach to working the program is unusual because I do not believe people need to say the word God when working the 12 Steps. I came to this viewpoint over the thirty years of my own recovery. In that time, I've constantly observed members, especially newcomers to the program and young people, who saw religious words as a barrier to working the Steps. Some self-identify as atheists or agnostics; others suffered harm in a religious institution or by clergy, or doubt the existence of a loving deity as a result of trauma.

I've also witnessed the myriad of ways that people who don't call God by name still practice faith. Some find their peace and grounding in nature; others in the warmth and acceptance of a supportive group. If this book can enable one person who feels constrained by religious language to recover from their disease using the Steps, then its purpose will be served. Though I speak primarily to readers who choose not to use the word "God" in their recovery, my goal is to be inclusive, not to discredit or offend any person or entity as related to 12-Step programs. I hope everyone on the recovery journey can gain something from this book. As we say in meetings, "Take what you like and leave the rest."

My experience with 12-Step programs has been positive and life-changing. My life is only one of the millions of lives that 12-

Step programs have transformed for the better. I have been clean and sober for three decades as a direct result of 12-Step programs.

What I have found through my experience of going to thousands of meetings, working in drug and alcohol treatment centers for over twenty years, and counseling individuals in early recovery, is that when some people think of a spiritual connection in broader terms than their religious affiliation—or the one their family practiced when they were children—they more fully connect with the program. I believe that what sets 12-Step programs apart from other spiritual programs is that you can "choose a god of your own understanding." Or, as I like to put it, "Choose a *power* of your own understanding."

Because AA was founded and influenced mostly by the Oxford Group, a Christian organization that helped alcoholics in the early 20th century, a lot of the language used in 12-Step literature is slanted towards Christianity. Through my experience, I offer an alternative spiritual approach. However, in no way do I intend to suggest that this book is an atheist text or a slam against any religious program. My belief and experience is simply that an individual can work the 12 Steps without using the word "God" or even choosing a "*god* of your understanding." Connecting with a "power greater than yourself" happens organically as a direct result of the work one does in the program towards achieving a new and different way of living.

One of the words I'll use throughout this book is the power of synergy: syn·er·gy, "the interaction or cooperation of two or more organizations, substances, or other agents to produce a combined effect greater than the sum of their separate parts." (Oxford Dictionary, 2018.) I believe that when a group of people works together for the greater good, there is massive power in that. I like to refer to that "power greater than ourselves" as synergy. As science confirms, everything in our universe is *energy*. Tapping into this positive energy through the process of helping other human beings,

I strongly believe, is the greatest gift one can give in this universe. Together, we experience synergy.

In the following pages, I will share with you a little history of my life experiences, speak to the disease model of alcoholism and addiction, talk about brain chemistry, touch on the origins of the 12 Steps, and give a clear and concise explanation of how my interpretations show you how to work the 12 Steps without naming God.

I will go through all the 12 Steps, providing an alternative way to examine them and potentially recover without using the word God. I'll reiterate that, for me, the 12 Steps is a program of action and of plugging into synergy—a power greater than yourself. My goal is to help you commit to a program of action, do the work and get a result. Let us not overthink this; by doing the work, you *will* get a result. And, as I've found, you do not have to self-identify as religious or spiritual to get there. So, if you are one of those individuals who have been put off by 12-Step meetings because of the religious undertones, especially if you had a negative experience with religion or the church, please know that you are welcome here. As is everyone.

By going through the process of working the steps, you *can* find some peace and serenity in your life. Maybe it's hard to imagine living your life without the horrors of your addiction, without the obsession to drink and use. I know that thirty years ago, I couldn't.

One thing I learned—and one of the biggest things I'd like you to remember going through the process of recovery—is that you do not have to go it alone. A huge part of a 12-Step program is that we do this together. The group synergy means that you never have to drink again or take drugs. You never have to be alone again if you choose this path. I promise you that. And that's true no matter what background you come from, no matter what's happened to you before. There is a path to recovery for everyone who wants to live a happier life.

No dogma here—my belief is in working the steps. Spirituality on its own will neither get you sober nor keep you sober. The power greater than yourself that grounds your recovery path comes from actually *working the steps*. Going through the process, going to meetings, and working with other alcoholics and addicts in recovery is the power—the synergy. The actions we take in alignment with 12-Step principles are the work that gets us results. If you make the commitment to do what is necessary, your life *will* be better. It has worked for me and thousands of other people.

This doesn't happen through osmosis and it doesn't happen overnight. Program old-timers aren't kidding when they tell you, "The one thing that you have to change is everything." Don't be daunted by that; they don't mean all of it at once. One step at a time, over a period of time, we work towards a greater good. Not just for ourselves, but for all whose lives we touch. I took my first steps thirty years ago and now I'm here to help you take yours.

David Vartabedian
Santa Barbara, California
2 February 2020

PROLOGUE: 1982

In L.A. in the 80s, Crenshaw and Adams was the corner of a not-so-great neighborhood. Driving by, you could see all the people hustling on the streets selling their drugs, their bodies and their souls.

I was often one of them. I sold and bought everything—cough medicine, Dilaudid, weed, cocaine, heroin. One night, my friend Ryan set up a deal for me to sell five pints of Citraforte cough medicine to some associates at Crenshaw and Adams with whom I had done business before. It was a mostly black neighborhood in the ghetto. Right down the street was an old, rundown apartment building where addicts, hookers, crackheads and dope fiends lived. One guy there was a relatively good friend of mine.

That night, Ryan drove me to the front of the apartment house. It was nearly nine o'clock at night in the winter when the days were getting shorter. I knew my associates were waiting for me and everything seemed normal. I lit up one of my Camel cigarettes and strolled down the alley next to the building. I saw the two guys standing there in the darkness.

In my mind, I can still see the cars in that alley. One was a 1977 Monte Carlo with Bondo primer paint on the rear fender. Another was up on blocks with no wheels on it. It looked like a junk yard back there.

It was dark out already but a light from one of the apartments above lit the parking lot, just barely. I could hear a couple arguing upstairs, most likely in a fight over drugs. A dog barked incessantly into the night, almost like a warning to me.

One of the guys I knew was smoking a cigarette and talking to another guy who was wearing a Members Only jacket. I walked towards them. "Hey, guys, what's going on? It's fucking cold tonight, huh?"

As I looked into their eyes, I could see that something was wrong but there was no time to react. Right then, I was hit over the back with a 2 x 4 and thrown to the ground. Then they put a knife to my throat and the one I considered a friend said to me, "*I will fucking kill you, motherfucker.*"

This is not where I wanted to die, in a dirty alley behind this shithole apartment building with my throat slit open, my blood gushing into the broken asphalt.

I wasn't ready for the rip-off. I had only brought one pint of cough syrup with me and left the other four in the car, because that is the way I did business. I had about $300 cash in my pocket; they rifled through it and took my money.

My so-called friend had his knee on my chest and the knife to my throat. He pushed the blade into my throat, stabbing me. In that moment, I felt the sensation of cold metal puncturing my throat and I wondered... *is this it? I could die right now.*

I felt blood gushing down my throat and all over my body. The two guys ran into the darkness.

Bleeding profusely, I barely made it back to Ryan's car. His face turned white as I fell into his ride. I looked down at my white shirt, which was now soaked in blood. I was bleeding so much, it was soaking into my blue jeans. I held my T-shirt up to my neck to try to stop it and instantaneously that shirt was drenched through with blood.

"Can you make it to the hospital, brother?" I asked Ryan, who looked like he was about to pass out.

We were next to the Santa Monica freeway, I knew the Kaiser Permanente hospital was just two exits down off La Cienega. Ryan rushed me to the E.R. We made up a story to the admitting nurse, saying we had pulled over to a liquor store off the freeway to buy a pack of cigarettes and we were jumped.

In the emergency room, the doctor worked to stop the bleeding. He said to me, "You're a lucky man tonight. If the knife had gone an eighth of an inch to the right, it would have severed your jugular vein. You would have bled to death in fifty seconds."

I felt lucky to be alive. I told him I was traumatized and in the next instant asked him if he would prescribe Valium and Dilaudid for me. You could tell he couldn't believe that came out of my mouth.

He looked at me with disgust and said, "Life on the street will kill you, kid. Whatever you're doing, *stop it.*" He did prescribe me some Valium, though. As soon as they released me, we sped to the closest drugstore. I grabbed the vial of pills, took ten of them and passed out in the car.

1

My Name Is David

CHAPTER 1

My Name Is David

My name is David. I'm an alcoholic.

I grew up in Southern California in the late 60s and 70s. My mother and father were wonderful people. As a child, I had no way of knowing what their demons were and how they would come to affect me, my brother, and four sisters. I knew that both my parents loved to drink, dance, and fight. I didn't know what alcoholism was. All I knew was that my mother drank and that she threw up a lot.

My mother was 100% Irish and my father was 100% Armenian. Our house was always passionate and filled with music, food, love and arguments. My father grew up on the East Coast, in Rhode Island, and my mother grew up in Virginia. That gives me a little bit of a Southern taste as well as a Yankee flavor.

Growing up, I watched my four sisters smoke cigarettes and listen to music. There was a lot of drinking going on with my older siblings, just as there was with my parents. There was a lot of drug experimentation, too. I just thought that our home reflected the society and times we lived in.

But something changed in the fall of 1969. My mother went to an alcohol treatment facility in downtown Los Angeles. I was thirteen years old. It was not what we know of addiction treatment today. Basically, it was a place where she could detox from alcohol, and not even a medical detoxification, just what was then called "drying out." I am not sure how long she was gone, but when she came home, she got involved with Alcoholics Anonymous and remained sober until her death in 1996.

With all those sisters in the house, I like to say I was raised by estrogen. The family dynamic was unusual; I was the youngest of six children and the only boy in the house until I was sixteen because in those years my one brother was living with his biological father.

While the family structure was a little complicated, the important thing is that it was all about my sisters and me. My parents loved us kids. It was complicated because my mother was married three times. Two of my siblings were from her first marriage, my brother, who was her firstborn, and one of my sisters. Another of my sisters was from her second marriage. My dad was her third marriage, which produced my two biological sisters and then, me. That made my half-brother and me (as they liked to say, "the baby of the family") bookends with the girls in the middle. My mother did get pregnant one more time, which would have given me a younger brother, but he was stillborn.

My mother had an interesting life. The biological father of her first two children was a country singer in the South. My mother was sixteen when my brother was born, and only a year or two older when she had my first sister. My mother's relationship with her then-husband, the country singer, was not working out. She and her man decided to go their separate ways. Over a pitcher of beer, they decided she would take the girl and he would take the boy. My brother didn't get to meet my mom until he was thirty-one years old.

My sister from her second marriage was an only child and I do not know much about her biological father, besides the fact my mom shared with me that he smoked a pipe.

She was still married to him when she met my father, who was serving in the U.S. Navy in San Diego, California, post-World War

II. She left her second husband to marry my dad and soon after became pregnant with the third and fourth "books" between her bookend sons.

My mother had a very strong personality and before AA her drinking was as heavy as it could possibly be. We did not have much money. In those days, we were living in Inglewood, California, a neighborhood in L.A.'s inner city. I shared a room with two of my sisters. My father had retired from the Navy and was working two jobs, driving a cab and trying to get started in the real estate business.

My mother worked, too. She was a barmaid at The Berkshire on Crenshaw in Inglewood. Sometimes after school, she would come and pick me up and take me back to work with her. I would have to sit in the bar and drink Shirley Temples or Roy Rogers until her shift ended. All I remember is that it was dark and the place smelled like bathroom cleaner and alcohol. It was like a scene out of The Days of Wine and Roses—all the women wore cocktail dresses; all the men wore suits and ties. The music was always Frank Sinatra, Ray Charles, and Johnny Mathis. It was pretty cool. Or maybe it was just really dysfunctional. I couldn't tell the difference.

It's funny, though; through all this, my mother was always protective of me, since I was the baby. Even though she was deep into her disease of alcoholism, I always had a sense that she was protecting me.

Before my mom finally got sober, the end of her drinking was really frightening. When she and my father were having a fight, I was so afraid that I would just put my head under the pillow and hope that it would go away. My mom was not okay, I knew, and neither was my dad. On some level I knew that they were in a very dysfunctional relationship. I remember one morning seeing my mom in the bathroom throwing up and trying to get vodka down into her system at the same time. It was traumatizing to me because I didn't understand it.

The weird, confusing thing was that both my parents had this functionality to them as well. All this fighting and all this drinking, then trying to put their best foot forward raising all these kids. I just remember being afraid a lot, and disconnecting from the scene when it got too scary and overwhelming.

My father was always very distant when I was growing up. He wasn't up to a lot of family activities. He worked very hard, sometimes seven days a week, and was exhausted when he got home. He usually just fell asleep right away. He was present sometimes— he was the coach of our Little League team. He wasn't totally absent. But we never really had those father and son heart-to-heart talks.

I always thought my dad was old-school East Coast with his Rhode Island upbringing near Federal Hill. Later in my life, I found out there was a lot of Mafioso in that area in his time and I wondered how the pieces of his life fit together.

I'm not sure if it was related or not but in his business dealings he seemed to have this kind of secret life. Everyone he knew carried a gun. I always thought it was because they carried a lot of cash and that the guns were for security. It seemed like his doings were not always on the up and up, and that he must have had connections to the underworld. He lived one life at home and another life in his business. The friends and associates of his that I met could look like a scene out of Goodfellas.

Don't get me wrong, my dad worked really hard in the real estate business and the day-to-day operations could be pretty much normal. But I grew up knowing that when something needed to be taken care of, there were other ways to do it besides the conventional method. I saw his associates use guns to evict people who were not paying rent from their homes, and not going through the proper channels to get them evicted. Once, someone tried to repossess my cousin's car for some reason. My father raced across the street and put a gun in the person's face, got him down on the ground and told him if he didn't get the fuck out of there he was gonna blow his face off.

What I remember most about my childhood is that I always felt different.

My mother's side of the family was never present. They were across the country and distant in other ways, too. I didn't know anyone in my mom's extended family; I never even met her parents, my grandmother and grandfather. Only later in my life did I finally meet her half-sister in Virginia.

The extended family that I knew was predominantly on my father's side. They, like my dad, were all 100% Armenian, whereas I was half Irish and half Armenian. One of the things I remember distinctly is that I wasn't allowed to go to Armenian school to learn the language because I was only half Armenian. All of my cousins went, which is why I felt like an outsider.

I never felt comfortable visiting my grandmother with all my cousins. There was always this fear that I had inside me, not knowing what it was. I loved going to the Armenian events and eating all the food, but I just felt a little out of place. (However, my cousin Johnny and I were born a month apart and we got along really well.)

School was another place I didn't fit in. When I was nine years old, we moved to Ranchos Palos Verdes, an upper middle class suburb of L.A. I had a weird last name in a predominantly white demographic. Most of the last names in Palos Verdes were Smith or Jones-like. Then, my mother held me back in the third grade, which made school even worse. I was always getting into fights, trying to defend myself being the oldest kid in class and being called stupid.

I felt like an outsider at home, too. My mother made all my older sisters look after me; there were never any babysitters in our house because we were all looking after each other. I did not feel like I fit in with my group of sisters; in fact, I felt like I was a major annoyance to them, like a gnat flying around their heads. If they were going to the park, or somewhere to get ice cream, my mother would always make them take me and they hated it. (I do not think they necessarily hated *me*, they just had a different agenda.)

With my dad working seven days a week to provide for my mom and all of us, and my older brother not yet on the scene, I really *was* immersed in a proverbial pool of estrogen. My sisters always talked about their problems without holding back. What I heard most as a kid were complaints; they would all say "I'm fat, I'm ugly and I have nothing to wear." It was odd to me because I didn't think they were fat or ugly and their closets had plenty of clothes.

I was pretty spoiled in the sense that I didn't have to do much in the way of cooking or cleaning or helping around the house. My old-school father thought women should do all the domestic work. My sisters hated that and thus nicknamed me "the little brat." They trained me from a young age to always put the toilet seat down; if I didn't, they'd beat me up. It's funny now, I live alone and I *still* put the dang toilet seat down.

My sisters would have fun sometimes, dressing me up as a girl. They thought it was hilarious. I learned to be very tolerant of their bright ideas and somehow the imprint of being around them all the time gave me malleability as I went through life. I can still see them doubled over in fits of laughter over how uncannily perfect my dress and makeup were, though to me it was not that funny. I never thought I made a very pretty girl. (And I was right: fast forward, 2004, going to a Halloween party dressed as a woman. As I was getting ready, I asked my then-wife "How do I look?" She said, "You look really scary. Take that off or you might get arrested. You look like the guy from Silence of the Lambs.")

By the time my sisters got to the age of having boyfriends over, I was in a position where I now had some leverage and they had to listen to what I said. My parents would go out dancing and partying and leave my sisters at home to babysit me. They were not supposed to have boys over, but they would bribe me with cool stuff like candy, ice cream, and sometimes even money to keep my mouth shut. It was awesome.

There was constant insanity in the dynamics between my father and sisters back then. Mood swings, always. That was another time I felt like I was watching from the outside.

My sisters would get in these crazy fights, mostly over the telephone, or getting time in the bathroom. One time, I remember my father coming up and ripping the telephone cord out of the wall because my sisters were fighting over it. I learned to sneak outside to pee because I could never get into the bathroom. When I did have a turn in there, it was always covered in nylons, clothes, makeup, curling irons, hair dryers; you name it, there was girl-stuff everywhere.

One great advantage of the estrogen pool was that each of my sisters had different interests in boys and in music and because of this, I developed a wide range of musical tastes. My older sister was all about Elvis and rockabilly, my second oldest sister was into the Beach Boys and surf music. My other two sisters loved Motown and Rock 'n Roll. One of them loved the Beatles, the other loved The Rolling Stones.

When my sister Darline got her license, and her first car, a 1967 Impala, the only thing that she was concerned with was, "Does the radio work?" I love that. She didn't ask how it ran, or how many miles it had on it, she cared about the radio! Music was a big part of our family, as you can see.

The way my sisters dressed was so cool. This was the late 1960s. It was all miniskirts, big hair-dos, and psychedelic-colored patterns. One of my sisters was into low-riding; her boyfriend had a '64 Impala. It was so low to the ground—literally, the height of a Marlboro pack off the ground.

My mom was constantly being called into the high school because my sisters' skirts were too short. She would take me along sometimes into the principal's office to talk about my sisters' dress code. (She always defended their looks and the style and fashion of the time. I thought it was awesome that she did that.)

My sisters loved me and hated me at the same time. Personally, I looked up to them and even in their dismissal of me, I still felt cared for and looked out for by them. We had our own dynamic and I know the estrogen pool I had at home growing up is the reason I get along with women so well today—I was raised by them. Thanks to my mother and sisters, I feel that I *know* women, I get them, I love them on a deep level.

I know my sisters had a different relationship with my mom than I did; I had special status both as the youngest and as the only boy in the pool. My mom was consistent about one thing with all of us, though. She was affectionate and always a big hugger. She would make sure she told us that she loved us regularly.

I took LSD for the first time when I was thirteen. That soon led to alcohol and other drugs. Maybe it was peer pressure. Maybe it was just curiosity. At some point, it was because I loved the feeling of being high.

As I got more involved with drugs, I began to distance myself from everyone in my family, emotionally and physically. I grew my hair long. (That caused Dad to ask Mom if I was gay.) My dad's military background of short haircuts made this a constant issue with him. Immediately after my junior high graduation, when my hair was at its longest, he took me straight to a barber. Then they took me to a psychiatrist.

They took me to a psychiatrist because my long series of bad choices had begun.

In school, I had always gravitated towards the misfits. That's where I was introduced to drinking and smoking weed. Plus, it was the times we were living in, the post-hippie movement. Music was a big part of my life—I've always loved to sing and still do to this day—and I looked up to a lot of musicians. In that time, we were listening to Black Sabbath, the Grateful Dead, Led Zeppelin, the Stones, all of them.

Within that music was a big drug culture that I thought was really cool.

I remember the first time I ever got high, my friends and I smoked hash. I don't think I felt it. All through high school, I drank alcohol, smoked weed and hash, and took a lot of LSD. We were surfers and skateboarders who loved to play music. My first band that I played with was called the Skull Mates. We'd play parties, drink and smoke weed. Drugs sent me to juvenile hall and then jail. I was kicked out of school several times.

I started dealing in marijuana, hash, LSD, reds (barbiturates) and whites (amphetamines). I learned early on that I could make money selling those drugs. It eventually turned into selling harder drugs. I never considered myself an alcoholic or an addict; it's just what everyone I knew was doing and I was making money doing it.

The irony was that my mother was now sober. I was never really close to her after that. She was deep in her AA program and it didn't seem like she was focused on the kids anymore. She made me a sack lunch every day. I would throw out the food and instead pack the sack with drugs that I would take to school and sell. As soon as I had sold everything that morning, I would leave school and go surfing with my friends.

I don't think I ever took any books out of my locker. My girlfriend would write papers for me; I'd be off getting high, drinking and surfing. One thing I do remember vividly from that time is that I would fall in love really hard. I think maybe it had something to do with really wanting that connection on a deeper level. I was deeply in love with my high school girlfriend. I'm not sure if all kids feel that way, but I sure did.

When I was seventeen years old and selling drugs out of the house, my mother asked me to move out. It almost caused a divorce with her and my father.

I didn't see my parents much after I left. I would connect with my father once in a while. My drug addiction escalated to consuming most of my life. Only once, when I was stabbed, did I go back to the house. My mom sometimes visited me in jail.

Things deteriorated fast. I remember my father coming to the house I was living in with some friends as we were cutting up a pound of cocaine. He walked in and I scrambled to cover up the coke on the dining room table with the newspaper. I don't think he knew what was happening. At that point, my garage was filled with hundreds of kilos of marijuana. I had just bought a brand-new BMW—with cash. I had tons of money and drugs.

My high school senior picture. Love those 70s!

My life was out of control, but in a functional way. I was running a dysfunctional pirate ship with a dysfunctional gang and loving it.

I wasn't ready or willing to do the work of sobriety. But when I finally was, my years in the family estrogen pool became a deep resource of experience, strength and hope. My mother used to tell me that I had emotional intelligence. I have a sense of easygoingness and flexibility that I believe comes from being raised in that highly feminine environment.

The image that comes to mind with all four of my sisters, my parents and me, is a home that was shaped like a volcano. There was a lot of chaos, heat, passion, and uncertainty. I was always wondering, when is it all going to blow to hell? But my character was formed and shaped by this chaos; I am convinced that this unpredictability gave me a certain inner strength and simultaneously the ability to change on a whim. My levels of patience and tolerance grew to be deep and wide. I was constantly trying to understand what was going on. I had to become a very good listener. I learned not to be judgmental. These all proved to be great tools in recovery.

The training I got from my mom and my sisters has also served me well in raising my daughter, who is now seventeen years old and an amazing young woman. I want to be a positive example in her life, and encourage her to connect with her highest self. We both love the arts, dance, music, theater, writing, reading, and poetry. I am a solid force in her life. She is going through her teenage stuff, plus a divorce between her mother and I, which has been tough on all of us. It is amazing to watch though how staying positive in the moment and not engaging in the insanity always helps. Everyone needs someone they can trust in and talk to. I try to be that for her.

I respect women's rights, I respect their voice. My mother was definitely pro-women, whether they were strong or weak, she used to say, she was for them. Two of my sisters have passed, as well as my older brother, so there's just three of us left. We live far away from each other, but we're still connected forever.

When my mom became sober and sponsored women in the program, I saw how much they respected her. She was the matriarch in her groups and she would do anything to help them if they were willing to do the work.

I know if there is a higher power, she is definitely a woman.

Recovery

CHAPTER 2
Recovery

A COMMON HISTORY

Alcoholic Anonymous was founded by people just like us, alcoholics. You might assume they had sobriety all figured out, but theirs was just as much a struggle for them as it has been for all of us. When a group of people called the Washingtonians started their movement in the 1800s, they were just a bunch of practicing alcoholics who saw how destructive alcoholism was and decided to try to help some people. Six alcoholics strong, they thought they could cure themselves and others of their alcoholism by relying on each other and sharing their struggle. The cornerstones of their movement were abstinence, faith, and community. And it worked... mostly. At one point, they had over 100,000 members, but the movement dissolved over time.

The Oxford Group was a religious organization in the 1900s that thought the answer to alcoholism was surrendering one's life to God. They came up with the idea that alcoholics take a personal inventory, admit their wrongs and ask for forgiveness as a path to sobriety. That worked, too.

It was the Oxford Group that helped Bill Wilson, one of the co-founders of AA, get sober (keep in mind, it took him several tries). Even then, those in the movement recognized the power in helping each other. However, Wilson—Bill W. in the "Anonymous" part of AA—found it was not easy helping other people get sober, even though the service he gave others supporting their recovery is what helped him stay sober. Bob Smith was the first person that Bill Wilson successfully helped to sobriety.[1]

Before the 12 Steps were developed and what we now know as the Big Book of AA was written, Bill W. and Bob S. created a 6-step program. Those steps included the following:

1) Complete deflation (what we now think of as "hitting bottom")

2) Dependence on and guidance from a higher power

3) A moral inventory

4) Confession

5) Restitution

6) Continued work with other alcoholics

Smith and Wilson designed AA based on the same principles that had worked for themselves and others in the past: surrender, abstinence, service and helping others who were in the same boat. Those are the same principles that have helped and continue to help millions of people get sober today. While "surrender" may have originally meant surrender to God, many members, including myself, think it has evolved into "*surrendering yourself over to the power of the 12-Step process.*"

AA's two founders both fell and got back up many times before they achieved sobriety. You can do it, too!

---

1   https://www.aa.org/pages/en_US/aa-timeline

THE DISEASE MODEL

You may already know that there has been a lot of controversy about whether alcoholism is a disease or a moral choice. In 1956, the American Medical Association recognized alcoholism as a disease. This opened the door to wider treatment options and helped to remove some of the stigma associated with alcoholism. Yet, some people still think of alcoholism as a weakness, a lack of willpower, and/or a bad habit. Let us examine the reality.

Alcoholism *is* a disease. What does that mean? In the Big Book of AA, the authors call it an allergy of the body, an obsession of the mind, and a spiritual malady. I'll talk about the spiritual malady aspect later in this chapter, but let's look first at what is an allergy and what is an obsession.

An allergy is having an adverse physical reaction to something. For example: if someone is allergic to bee stings, they could die from one. Someone who is allergic to strawberries could break out in hives or their throat could swell shut. So, if someone has an allergy to alcohol, it means they have an adverse physical reaction to it. Think of it as you would a diabetic. Their body cannot regulate insulin levels, so when a diabetic eats too much sugar their body has an adverse reaction, whereas non-diabetics do not.

When a non-alcoholic person drinks, in most cases, they know when they've had enough. They know when to stop. Think of a thermostat. Most people have an internal thermostat for alcohol in place—when they hit a certain "temperature," they stop. However, when an alcoholic takes a drink, it triggers what they call the "phenomenon of craving." In other words, their thermostat is broken. An alcoholic has lost the ability to enjoy and control their drinking.

An obsession of the mind can be defined as an unreasonable and continually recurring idea. Such a fixation on alcohol occurs even when an alcoholic or addict is *not* actually drinking. They become *restless, irritable,* and *discontent* until they can achieve the ease and comfort that comes from taking a few drinks or using drugs. This is a dysphoric state, the opposite of euphoria. When dopamine and endorphins are completely depleted, brain chemistry is altered and you are in a dysphoric state.

Alcoholics have a predisposition to their disease. This can be a genetic predisposition, as is certainly true for me, or what some people call "nature." There are also environmental factors, referred to as "nurture." There is a lot of debate about how much of alcoholism is nature vs. nurture, but in my own experience, it seems to be about 45 percent nature and 55 percent nurture. This means that if your family history predisposes you genetically to alcoholism, if you start drinking you'll have about a 45 percent chance of having an adverse physical reaction to alcohol. If your family had a history of heart disease, you would also have a higher chance of having it, too. The 55 percent nurture means your upbringing (environment) or life experiences also contribute to your chances of becoming an alcoholic. That was true for me, too.

Let's talk about brain chemistry. An alcoholic or addict has a different brain chemistry or chemical imbalance than non-alcoholics do. When it comes to drugs and alcohol, a normal drinker can take it or leave it. Alcoholics feel compelled to take it and keep on taking it.

When I worked at Klein Bottle, a drug and alcohol treatment center for high-risk youth in Santa Barbara, I went to a week-long training seminar on drugs and their effects on brain chemistry. Dr. Alex Stalcup, a national addictions expert who runs the New Leaf Treatment Center in Oakland, California, shared his research on the effects that drugs and alcohol have on the mind. He stated that if an individual consumes drugs or alcohol daily for a period of six months or longer, that individual has altered their brain chemistry, depleting their dopamine, endorphins, and serotonin.

When an individual takes drugs and/or alcohol, it mimics the effects of these brain chemicals and, over time, the brain learns to produce less of them.

One of my questions for Dr. Stalcup was, "Does that mean anyone can become an alcoholic or alter the chemistry of their brain?" His response was, "Yes, that statement is true," but he added that most non-alcoholics will not ingest drugs or alcohol on a daily basis for a period of six months or longer. He also reiterated that alcoholism and drug addiction is, in fact, a brain disease.

Dr. Stalcup spoke about neurotransmitters and just *how* drugs and alcohol affect the brain. I learned that the brain naturally produces endorphins and/or dopamine. Endorphins are the body's natural pain relievers. For example, what we call a "runner's high" happens when an individual starts running and the brain releases endorphins because it feels that the body is in pain. Dopamine is the chemical released when something good happens in your life, like when you get a good grade on a test or you win a soccer match. You feel happy or excited when your brain releases dopamine. This is what produces a euphoric state. Serotonin is the natural emotional stabilizer. It creates balance and harmony for the rest of the neurotransmitters.

Because the use of drugs and/or alcohol mimics the effects of this brain chemistry, they "tell" the brain that it does not need to produce these chemicals on its own anymore. In essence, drugs trick the brain to stop making endorphins because the drugs are supplying them.

Another example of this would be when a male or female bodybuilder uses steroids or testosterone, and the body stops producing testosterone. Then, when the bodybuilder stops using it, his or her body craves it. It's the same with an alcoholic or addict—when they stop drinking/using, they go into a state of dysphoria until they use again. This state of restlessness, anxiety, and uneasiness is caused by the fact that the body now craves these feel-good chemicals but doesn't provide them. It's just like the diabetic who has a physical reaction to sugar that needs medical intervention. People can also be "addicted" to sugar. Just like alcohol, sugar mimics a dopamine high in the body, and if someone replaces actual dopamine with sugar for long enough, they will suffer without it. An alcoholic suffers when they do not get enough sugar/alcohol.

Here's another way to see it: imagine that you are looking at a scale, with a zero in the middle as "normal," (which is different for everyone); ten is euphoria and minus ten is dysphoria. When the brain releases dopamine, creating excitement and a sense of well-being… when someone starts using drugs, smoking a joint or having a drink, the brain is now mimicking that sense of well-being or euphoria that once came from something wonderful and natural like winning a game or falling in love. The scale moves toward ten. The stronger the drugs, the greater the depletion of endorphins and dopamine in the brain, until eventually, the brain no longer produces these chemicals. The scale moves toward minus ten. Now, you have to use drugs and/ or alcohol just to get to a "normal" state of mind, or zero. The brain has now achieved "neuro-adaptation" or tolerance.

Let us talk some more about dysphoria. Say that you've been using drugs and alcohol for one, ten or twenty years and your brain has been robbed of all the good brain juice. Once you stop using, you experience dysphoria, which is basically: sobriety sucks. Or as the Big Book of AA puts it, you are "restless, irritable and discontent." So, at this point, all one can think about in early sobriety is: "I know what will fix this problem, to get me into not even euphoria, but just a normal state of being—alcohol!" Does this sound (or feel) familiar? The physical craving is intense. It may even feel overpowering.

I know what you're thinking, that maybe you've fucked up your brain chemistry forever and it's never going to recover. But the exciting piece of information is that if you're willing to do the work, take direction, and show up to your life, you will be amazed at how well the brain *can* recover. Your brain will recover; you'll be able to produce dopamine, serotonin and endorphins naturally again. By working out, along with self-enhancement practices like yoga, meditation, creating art, working the Steps, leading a healthy lifestyle and being in a gathering of like-minded people who share your goal of recovery, you can encourage your brain to again produce dopamine, endorphins and serotonin.

The act of working with a fellow addict is so powerful, it *fundamentally changes their brain chemistry*. This is where doing an action contrary to what we might believe works is applicable. One person's recovery helps lift everyone's. We can cause this to happen by aligning ourselves with the loving and compassionate energy that is present in this universe—the contrary action to what we did before in our lower-vibrational energetic state, which was drink or use.

Again—I want to stress this—let's not overthink this; do the action and get a result. Or, as Bill W. said, "You cannot think your way into the right action, you need to *act your way into the right thinking.*"

When I was in the throes of my disease, I would wake up every morning and say, "I gotta get well because I feel sick." That's what it felt like to be in a dysphoric state. It wasn't even about getting high, it was about getting well or normal.

I've stated this before but I want to emphasize this, too: positive actions like physical exercise (e.g., yoga or working out), eating right, going to meetings, and working with another addict or alcoholic all create synergy, or a new way of being. That in turn re-stimulates the release of the wonderful dopamine and endorphins in your brain.

SPIRITUALITY

The 12-Steps literature speaks a lot about spirituality. In particular, Step Twelve says, "Having had a spiritual awakening as the result of the Steps, we tried to carry the message to other alcoholics, and practice these principles in all our affairs." I believe we really must investigate what a spiritual awakening is, because all 12-Step programs suggest that this is the cure or treatment for alcoholism and/or addiction.

Since the beginning of time, people have had what they call spiritual experiences or spiritual awakenings. In the Big Book of AA, Dr. Carl Jung, the iconic Swiss psychiatrist who founded analytical psychiatry, gives his description of a spiritual awakening. He describes it as "[I]deas, emotions and attitudes which were once the guiding forces of the lives of these men are suddenly cast to one side and a completely new set of conceptions and motives began to dominate them." (From the Big Book of Alcoholics Anonymous, page 27).

In my experience, a spiritual awakening takes place over a period of time. It's like peeling an onion. There are layers that you must go through to get to the essence of understanding and feeling the synergy. As you get deeper into your recovery, more and more of your inner layers are revealed. It almost seems like things are revealed to you just as you're ready to process them, just as when the student is ready, the teacher appears. The more rituals you do daily to penetrate your inner life, the more that understanding them becomes an organic part of your life, integrated into the whole of your being. You are awakening.

As it is written in the Spiritual Experience appendix in the Big Book of AA, "Most of our experiences are what the psychologist William James calls the 'educational variety' because they develop slowly over a period of time." (The Big Book of AA, page 569).

Here's a comparison to what a spiritual awakening over a period of time feels like:

A lot of people buy memberships to gyms. When they actually get to the gym and start to work out, they find out that it's a process that takes a lot of commitment. You start with lighter weights and work up to heavier weights. You do not just jump on the treadmill and go for an hour, you start with fifteen minutes. *It's a process.* The important thing is consistency. Suit up, show up and you *will* get results. In a spiritual awakening, insights and periods of peace come upon you gradually as you do the work of self-reflection and being part of the recovery community. You come to know yourself so well and see progress in others so consistently that you build on the spiritual connection, which grounds your experience, strength and hope.

I recently read this next quote, which is a great example of practical application: do the work, get a result:

"If we study but do not practice, we will not get results. It's like a man who raises chickens but does not collect the eggs. All he gets is the chicken shit. To get the best results you must study and practice as well." (So wrote Thai Buddhist monk and meditation teacher Ajahn Chah, in *Food for The Heart: The Collected Teachings of Ajahn Chah.*)

When working the Steps leads you to a spiritual awakening, you're relieved of the obsession to drink or drug. By changing your actions and also taking contrary action, you've tapped into a power greater than yourself, one that has worked for so many. There is an absolute power in doing this; you're living by a set of new principles in your life, a design for living fueled by something bigger than you. You're aligning yourself with a loving and positive energy. *This happens by doing the work and getting a result.* Continuing to tap into that power greater than yourself by sharing this message with other suffering alcoholics and addicts will also serve you well. Again: "*One cannot think their way into the right action, one must act their way into the right thinking.*"

Take the appropriate action and get a different result. Simple, right? But it all depends on you. While I'm sure that some people have what we call a spiritual experience like the burning bush or a vision, for most people spiritual awakening comes over time by working on themselves. No sea parts, no one lays hands on you, you're not accepting anyone as your personal savior. *This is a practical application of a program of action.* The thing I still must constantly remember is: this is not a one-off. (Yes, even after thirty years of sobriety! One day at a time.) What keeps me connected to that power greater than myself, that synergy, *as well as* treating my alcoholism, is continuing to carry this message and practicing these principles in all my affairs. *Love and service.* If you stay connected to this positive energy in this universe, you can live your life with this higher meaning and purpose.

I am continually energized by taking the action, doing the Steps, and working with other alcoholics and addicts. Doing things for others and not wanting anything in return is probably the greatest feeling I have ever felt. There is nothing more enlightening and rewarding than doing altruistic work.

They say in the 12-Steps literature that this selfless service can bring you to a personal relationship with your higher power. It's true, though, that many people have their own concept of what a higher power is. Step work connects you with yours.

Throughout my life, I've been very interested in world religions and history. I was drawn towards the Eastern religions, particularly Buddhism. However, you do not have to pick a religion or spiritual program. For me, it just sort of happened. I started doing the work, going to meetings, working with my sponsor, expanding my meditation practice, and working with other alcoholics and addicts. I not only saw a change in myself, but I felt it every day. I still do. I have been doing this practice daily for thirty years. It works, it really does.

AA is living by a set of 12 principles. Here I have broken them down into one word each, Step by Step, as laid out by Alcoholics Anonymous:

Step 1 - Honesty

Step 2 - Hope

Step 3 - Faith

Step 4 - Courage

Step 5 - Integrity

Step 6 - Willingness

Step 7 - Humility

Step 8 - Love

Step 9 - Justice

Step 10 - Perseverance

Step 11 - Spirituality

Step 12 - Service

Continuing the work, spreading the love, I believe, is all you must do. You'll find that things that worked for you when you were drinking and using will now become obsolete. They're just no longer comfortable for you to partake. When you plug into positive energy, the negative things that were in your life will simply no longer work for you.

For example, when I got out of prison—I'm embarrassed to admit this—I was dismayed to find I'd become a racist there. Prison is completely structured in segregation and not adhering to the racial rules means bodily harm or even death. In that environment, my utter survival depended on playing by those rules; it was like an armored suit used to protect my very being. Once I was living again in normal society, trying to assimilate back into it, I had to go through a process of letting go of that sinister hatred, judgment, and defensiveness. I had to relearn how to walk around daily without this aggression. The program taught me how to lay down that armor, piece by piece.

Lying, cheating, manipulating, racism, bigotry, greed… these did not happen in me overnight and this was not flimsy armor. Slowly, I began having what they refer to as the "educational variety" of a spiritual awakening. I retrained my worst impulses by doing the work, practicing the Steps, applying the principles, going to meetings, and working with others. Anything learned can be unlearned. In fact, most of the behaviors when you're drinking and using are not genetic (even if you are genetically predisposed). Most of these behaviors are learned.

THE POWER OF THE TRINITY

What we call the Trinity in AA is Recovery, Unity and Service. When all three of those are plugged in, you've tapped into a power greater than yourself—the synergy.

The Recovery part of the Trinity is working the 12 Steps, the foundation of your program. The power you get from working with your sponsor and other recovering alcoholics is paramount.

Unity is going to meetings and networking with other alcoholics/addicts who have sobriety as a common goal. There is a lot of power in 12-Step meetings. You can feel the love and camaraderie. People are there to help and to be helped.

Service is what we give back to the program. Whether it be in commitments at meetings, volunteering in hospitals or jails, sponsoring individuals, taking people through the Steps, or just simply giving someone a ride to a meeting or being a good listener, anything to support the program is service. All of this to me is hugely spiritual. When I sponsor an individual in the program, I ask one thing: they must promise me that if I take my time helping them through the 12 Steps they will, in return, pay it forward by helping someone else. That is it. No money or future payment. We tap into the power and give it away. We keep it flowing. Love and service. That is all!!! A power greater than ourselves. Synergy.

As an example of the power of synergy, which shocks even me from time to time, although I lived through it, I will tell you this story of another time of my life. It almost feels like an account about another person. Sometimes I say to myself, "I cannot believe this was me." I'm not a better or worse person now, I'm simply living in a different energy field. I know that sounds weird, but I'm living by a new set of principles and it puts me into a higher vibration, connected to my higher self. When I am helping others, being kind, compassionate, loving and giving, I'm living in a higher vibration. When I am being resentful, fearful, selfish and act out according to these feelings, that's my lower-vibrational self. The contrast is… well, you'll see.

MY STORY: HITTING BOTTOM, CHOOSING RECOVERY

People used to ask me, "What's your drug of choice?" My response was always the same: "Whatever you'll front me." I was most fond of opiates, including heroin, morphine, hydrocodone, loads, cough medicine with codeine, or whatever you could front me.

During the middle to late 70s and into the early 80s, my friends and I were totally into these cough medicines called Tussinex and Citraforte. We would forge prescriptions, hustle doctors, and bribe pharmacists with shitloads of money to get what we wanted. We would do whatever it took to hustle. We would get it from the pharmacies and then sell it in the ghettos. At one point, we had great connections where we could buy it by the gallon and would sell pints for $100 bucks. I had one pharmacist who would sell me 1,000 Dilaudid (hydromorphone) pills at a time and I would then sell one pill for $25 or 100 at $15 a piece.

There was another drug we'd get called "loads." It consisted of four Codeine number 4 pills and two Doriden, which is a sedative that was used for insomnia in the 1950s. Someone figured out that the combination of these two drugs produced an opiate-like high.

The high they produced was amazing—warm with the sensation of floating. I didn't have a care in the world. When I felt it coming over me, any pain—physical, emotional, or spiritual—would just melt into the background.

But it was cough medicine that got me stabbed in the throat in 1982. After the two guys jumped me in the alley, stole my $300, slashed my throat and took off in the darkness, my friend Ryan saved my life by driving me to the Emergency Room. The last thing I remember about that night was swallowing the ten Valiums in Ryan's car. After that, I was out like a light. At which point, Ryan didn't know what to do with me. I must have scared him so much that he freaked out thinking I was going to die and my parents ought to know, so he brought me to their house.

That's where I woke up: in my parents' house. This was really weird because I hadn't lived there in years. I was bandaged up from head to toe.

That morning—this is the odd part—I happened to wake up during my mother's weekly women's AA meeting. This bunch of ladies got together at noon one day a week at her house to work out of the Big Book of AA. *This* is where I woke up from having a near-death experience, out of a state of unconsciousness. I *literally* came to *in an AA meeting*!

If that wasn't the universe hitting me over the head with a 2 x 4, I do not know what it was.

The women called their weekly meeting "The God Squad." Besides studying the Big Book, they would pray together for their children or other drug addicts and alcoholics they knew.

Fully awake now, I walked out of my old bedroom (my clothes were gone so I grabbed a robe that was way too small; it looked like a mini skirt) and looked over the top of the stairs.

The entire group of ladies looked back at me, and said things like, "Honey, I'm so glad you're awake," and "Can we get you something to eat?"

These women were the sweetest people in the world. My mom was relieved her son was alive.

This is an example of what I mean by the power of synergy. This is what happens when you get together in a group of two or more for the greater good. When you come from love, compassion, forgiveness, and service to others, wanting nothing in return, we tap into an energy, the "synergy."

These women with their prayer and meditation were sending positive energy into the universe. The constant belief and faith in a power greater than themselves, I believe, is what kept me alive after being stabbed in the throat behind a crackhead apartment building. It might sound weird, and you might be wondering: why did other people have to die in situations like that and not me? I cannot answer that question. All I know is that my mother's group of women were putting out love, compassion and positive energy into the universe. She and her friends were praying together. Whatever you want to call it, they had tapped into a higher power.

But I still didn't come to accept any of this until years after I was stabbed that night behind the crack house. Even regaining consciousness in an AA meeting in my mother's house wasn't enough to set me on the path to recovery. Yet.

Looking back, the events that led me into addiction began even before I got into drugs in high school.

When we moved from Inglewood to Palos Verdes, we went from being poor to being well-off. The culture shock was such that I was amazed that schools had grass in the yard; in the inner-city, all playgrounds were strictly asphalt. My dad had started to do very well in real estate and the good times meant lots of parties (and alcohol) at our house. There were cocktail parties and all my mom's and dad's friends would be there. Everyone dressed to the nines. I would always sneak a couple of drinks or sips, nothing crazy. I just liked the taste.

My parents had a tradition of going out dancing and drinking every Friday night. Then they'd come home and have knockdown, drag-out brawls. The fights were insane. Furniture crashing, nearly breaking, them screaming at the top of their lungs. I've told you how frightening that was for me.

One Friday night when my parents were out, something significant happened in my life. I saved someone else's life.

I was about nine years old. This kid, Sean, and I snuck over to the fields across the street from my house just to horse around. The fields were tall with green grass. It was still late winter in Southern California; spring hadn't arrived yet. There was a chill in the air and we both had on Levi's and heavy jackets, though our Chuck's Converse sneakers quickly got soaked from playing in the wet grass. One of our favorite games was dirt-clod hand grenades or stick fights. I always left welts on my friend's legs and my mom used to get mad at the scratches on my body and my ripped clothing.

On this one night, it was just starting to get dark. The temperature quickly dropped and my eyes started to water and my hands numbed up. Sean and I were just gathering up our belongings to head home when I heard, "Pssst! Hey, over here!"

Moving through the tall grass, we heard someone quietly calling out to us. It was a young girl's voice so I immediately looked around.

We heard it again. "Pssst! Please help me!"

"Psst!" I hissed. "Where are you?"

"Over here!"

You couldn't see anyone because the grass was so tall and it was getting darker by the second. We finally made our way over to her by crawling through the grass. There she was, a six or seven-year-old girl, crying.

She told us, "I was kidnapped by a bad man. I'm from Long Beach, California. My name is Rachel and he pulled over to go to the bathroom and that is when I got away."

My initial response was, "Do not worry. We'll get you out of here. I'll protect you. Just shh! And stop crying."

Long Beach was about twenty miles away—so this man had kidnapped Rachel and was planning to do God knows what to her. We lay there in the tall grass quivering with fear. It took everything for me to hold still and not pee my pants. We were trying not to breathe.

Now we could hear him circling around and abruptly he yelled out, "Get back here! I'm not going to hurt you!"

I was scared to death for all three of us. It was completely dark by then and he was only ten or twenty feet from us. I was holding onto Rachel and Sean, doing my best to hinder their breathing while she was trying not to cry. Finally, he got back in the car and drove around in circles. Just as I thought it was safe to get up, he stopped again and got out of the car. We heard him coming towards us, calling Rachel's name. This time, he stomped through the grass so close he almost stepped on us.

Finally, after what seemed like hours, he got back into his car and drove off.

We ran as fast as we could back to Sean's house and told his parents everything that had just happened. I knew in my bones that if that man had found us, he would've killed us all.

My parents were still out on their Friday Date Night. Sean's parents called the police and they interviewed the three of us. I remember the officer looking me straight in the eye and saying to me, "You know, you saved this girl's life, you're a hero."

We were featured in the Palos Verdes newspaper as local heroes. The pastor at our church was quoted in the story and he wrote me a letter commending me for the actions I took to protect this little girl. I had acted out of instinct, I would have done that for anyone.

Later, when I got into trouble and started using drugs, I went to the same pastor and asked him if he would write me a letter to help me get a less severe prison sentence. He did write the letter but I remember him looking at me, not as he looked at me from before, but with complete disgust. When he hugged me after I had helped a little girl, I remember the light in his eyes. That light had gone out and I felt like a piece of shit.

I was hardcore-addicted to opiates, heroin and prescription medication, all of it, by my late teens.

I knew about AA from my mother, but I did not believe I had a problem. Just as she started her recovery, smoking pot became a daily occurrence for me, as well as drinking beers, while hanging out and surfing. My mother was very religious even in her disease and would take us to the Baptist church, where we would sing hymns and learn about the Bible. So, I'd always known about God and the teachings of Jesus Christ. Though I didn't have a negative view of the church and its teachings, I did question some of the literal translations of the Bible. Ultimately, I don't have a bias. (I am sharing this to let *you*, the reader, know that we do not need to get caught up in the dogma of the literature.)

Strung out on opiates, I went into my first treatment facility in San Pedro, California at age 21. There, I detoxed and was introduced to AA as well as Narcotics Anonymous (NA). I didn't stay clean and sober though, during that first attempt at treatment. I continued to drink and use drugs full-throttle. Several times, I was arrested and spent time in the county jail, which taught me how to play the prison game. Something inside me started to shut down. I unintentionally constructed an emotional barrier around me just to survive there. And it was a game of survival of the fittest.

By the late 70s and early 80s, I was so severely addicted that I was in and out of treatment centers *and* jails. Dealing drugs eventually landed me in the state prison. Once, during the 1980s, I put together sixty days of sobriety by going to meetings. However, I ended up spending most of the mid- to late-80s in state prison for robbery as well as drug-dealing.

Meanwhile, my mom was now sober but my dad was in legal trouble.

He had always provided for his family. He had always put his family first. He was a guy who would sleep on the floor so his kids could have a bed. He would have given his children his last dollar so they could eat.

He joined the Navy when he was seventeen and retired at thirty-seven. He was in eleven major conflicts in the South Pacific. He was a decorated veteran. He was a businessman as well as a real estate broker. I learned so much from him. But, as I would discover, he had demons, too.

In 1986, my crimes landed me in Los Angeles County Jail. There are over 5,000 people in that jail. When you arrive, they take you to the basement, which has several holding cells. There, you wait to be processed and then sent upstairs to your housing unit. As I shuffled down the corridor in chains, my wrists and ankles aching from the steel digging into my skin, they steered me towards the holding cells. I happened to glance into one of the cells on my right and I froze. My father was sitting right there on the ground in front of me.

I was overwhelmed with emotion to see the man I knew as the rock in my life sitting on the floor of the L.A. County Jail, looking beaten down and defenseless. My dad would never back down to anyone; he was always the protector and I had seen him go toe-to-toe with some of the toughest characters. The discordancy of this was too much for me and a wave of nausea came over me.

"Dad!," I shouted. The guard shoved me from behind with force and told me to keep moving. All I could get out was, "Listen for your last name and they'll put us in the same dorm!"

I had to keep moving through the dungeons of this medieval-like castle with the sounds of chains clanking, cell doors slamming, and people screaming and crying. The stench was overwhelming.

I knew my dad had been in jail in Chino for real estate fraud but I wasn't exactly sure when he was being shipped to Terminal Island Federal Penitentiary in L.A. County.

When you are processed at the L.A. County Jail, they house you in the dorms for several days or weeks, depending on how full the jail is. Afterwards, they assign you to a cellblock.

My father's health was not in good shape. He'd had a stroke in 1984, partly because of the stress from real estate-related court cases. When they sent me upstairs to the housing unit called 9500 dorms, in the 9000 block of the county jail, I realized my father had not heard his name, so we were not placed in the same dorm. What the hell had happened to him? Where was he? Now I was worried sick.

The jail was so crowded that all they could do is move bodies around. You could be transferred from one part of the jail to another at any given moment. You could never fully settle in or relax there because they are always moving you and circumstances seem to change from one moment to the next. Everything is suspect and dangerous due to the instability in there. It's a madhouse.

I spent one eternal day in the 9500 block before they transferred me to the 9400. As soon as they opened the door to let me in, I saw my father sitting on one of the bunk beds. He was with a bunch of guys from an L.A. street gang; one of the city's biggest, they controlled drugs and organized crime on the streets. I was so happy and so horrified at the same time to see him sitting there. His poor health was more pronounced now. He had been robbed downstairs in the holding cells; they had taken everything he had in his possession, including his shoes. The guys in the gang had given him a pair of shower shoes tagged with their insignia.

I knew one of the guys; I'd dealt drugs with him on the street. I told him how grateful I was (and I am, to this day) that they took care of my father and gave him a pair of shoes. We shot the shit for a little while, and then I found a bunk bed for us to share. My dear father was so tired and so sick. We only had about two weeks together before I was shipped off to Chino to do my state time. I "caught the chain before him" and he was sent off to federal prison for his evaluation. He had been involved with a real estate development project with bankers and mortgage companies and the project went south. The group made decisions that were against the law and my dad landed in prison.

Sometimes, I learned what to do from my dad and sometimes I learned what not to do. He took some big risks and made some bad decisions. It was heart-wrenching to see him in this vulnerable position. He had always protected me. Now I wanted to protect him.

There are three systems in jail or prison. The first is County Jail, second is State Prison and third is Federal Prison. My father had to do a short term for the state of California as well as the Federal government. He was housed in Chino State penitentiary and then Terminal Island. In the transition from state to federal prison, the standard practice is to first take the prisoner back to the county jail. Once you're in county jail, the feds pick you up and take you to Terminal Island. My dad had already served out his state prison time in Chino.

I was in the L.A. County jail after being transported from the San Luis Obispo County Jail. They picked me up on felony warrants for prescription forgery, as well as sales of cocaine and heroin. For me, at the time, that was minor stuff. But L.A. County Jail has it all: fighting, stabbing, robbery, rape. It is one of the craziest facilities I've ever done time in.

They sent both me and my dad to Wayside Max, the highest security of all the county facilities, on our way to the penitentiary. It was the weirdest thing in my life to do time with my father. Obviously, I had mixed emotions. I was happy I was there to help him but also very sad that our lives had come to this.

I knew a lot of guys when I got to Wayside Max. In prison, as I've said, everything is racially segregated. Whites stay with whites, blacks stay with blacks, Mexicans stay with Mexicans. A few of my friends from Long Beach saved a place in the dorms for us. Every morning, I would make my dad's bed, help him to the bathroom, walk with him to the chow hall. We would sit and laugh and play cards with my homeboys. The dorms were filled with the Aryan Brotherhood, Black Gorilla Family and Mexican Mafia (La Eme). Northern Mexicans were placed outside of the dorm.

You're allotted fifteen minutes on the phone and there's a sign-up sheet that the correctional officers manage. I was signing up for the phone one day, and I asked if I could put my father's name down to get him fifteen minutes as well, so we could call my mother back-to-back.

The correctional officer said, "You're in here with your father? Wow, he did a great job."

I responded with, "Fuck you! You do not know anything about my father." That's all it took for them to get me into another room and give me "flashlight therapy." I had some major bruises on my head; nothing to the face because they do not want it to show.

When I went back to the dorm where my father and all my homeboys were, a wave of sadness washed over me. I had always seen my father as the strongest man in the world but here he was pretty beaten down. I'm glad I was able to take care of him for that brief time. The day I shipped out to the state pen, I had to leave my father. I was pretty choked up holding back the tears and just hoping his journey would be safe.

It would turn out that my dad was with me in a sense. A few days after I'd arrived at the Chino Prison Processing Center, I was greeted by one of the inmates handing out bedding. He said to me, "You're Pop's son. We knew you were coming. Everything will be taken care of for you."

I was sent to my cell, which was everything you might imagine, just like out of a movie. The cell block is three or four tiers high; the smell of body odor, shit, burning plastic and more shit, including cow shit from the nearby dairy farm, would just kill you. Men were screaming and yelling, you saw fires from their cigarettes and matches coming out of their cells. The scene was straight out of the movie American Me.

When I got to my cell, I lay down on my bunk thinking, "How the fuck did this happen to me? I'm in prison and there's nothing I can do to get the fuck out of here." I was morose. Here I was, just a kid, a surfer from suburbia who had landed in one of the worst places on earth. A living hell.

A few hours passed. Then, someone came to my cell and handed me a pack of cigarettes and some instant coffee through the bars.

The guy said, "This is from friends of your father." It was like I was in the fucking Mafia. My "celly," who shockingly turned out to be kind of fucking crazy, said to me, "You must have some juice in here. You must be somebody. No one gets cigarettes on the first day."

After a few days, they transferred me to the West Yard at Chino. Chino West Yard is different from Chino Central. Chino Central is only prison cells; Chino West Yard is dormitories. When you're housed in the West Yard you go for a psychological evaluation.

They have a system to evaluate your points to determine your level of custody.

The first day in West Yard, the same thing happened. Two guys came up to my bunk, with a carton of cigarettes, coffee, some candy bars, and a camp jacket.

"Do not worry about a thing," one said. "This is from friends of your father." I was a little nervous not knowing who these people were but what was I going to do?

A few more days passed. One morning, I was walking the yard with one of my homeboys. As I passed the bleachers, five or six older men waved me over. They asked me how I was doing, was I okay? I said, yes, I was fine and I thanked them for everything they had done. They told me what a great guy my father was and told me again that I didn't have to worry about anything. They asked me if my mother was coming to visit me. I said I thought so.

Then the weirdest thing happened.

At that time, I had long hair and a Fu Manchu mustache. One of the guys, Tony, said, "Why don't you cut your hair for your mother?"

I thought, wow, do I *have to* cut my hair? Now that I'm in prison with a bunch of clean-cut Mafia gangsters, *now* I have to cut my hair? How ironic. I just kind of laughed and changed the subject. From then on, every day I would see them in the yard and I'd say hello. Every few days one of them would give me a package of different things like Zoo Zoos and Wham Whams (look that up in your urban dictionary).

After a couple of weeks, I was transferred to Susanville, which was the furthest prison in Northern California at that time. I heard there was a lot of rioting; people were very tense because it was far away and no one was getting visits. If people do not get visits, there are not a lot of drugs in the yard. That causes tension.

I often wondered: why did I have to go through all of this?

Some people say it has made me a stronger human being. Who fucking knows? We all have our own journeys and this was mine. My parents each had theirs. Mine is linked with theirs; I know that.

In the ensuing years, when I was sober, I was able to take care of my father. When my mother died in 1996, she made me promise I would take care of him. She said I was the only one of all of the siblings who could do it. Our roles were reversed. My father died in 2005 and up until that point, I could care for him and make sure he was okay. During those last nine years of his life, my father saw his son become a responsible human being living a spiritual life. I cannot say it wasn't tough at times, taking care of him, but it was an honor to do it. For everything that he had done for me that I could, at last, change the energy and be a loving, responsible, caring son. Rest in paradise, Dad.

During my time in prison, I never stopped using. I would be released and go right back to what I was doing before. I knew it was not the right thing to do but I couldn't stop my disease.

In 1989, I was back doing more time in state prison. That is when I had what they call "a moment of clarity." I was under the influence of heroin (yeah, you can get drugs in prison). As I stood on the tier looking over the prison yard, I suddenly, spontaneously knew with certainty that something had to change.

I vowed to myself, "I will do whatever it takes to change my life."

That was July 7, 1989. The next day I woke up sober. That was my sobriety date: July 8, 1989. I have had continuous sobriety to this day. That day, I had a year to go on my sentence. My release date was scheduled to be July 11, 1990. From my sobriety date on, the obsession to drink and use was lifted. Something shifted in my energy and I was able to focus on the positive aspects of my life going forward. It was a stunning moment of clarity twenty years in the making.

For the rest of that year, I did my time going to meetings in prison as well as at the prison fire camp I was transferred to. My mother would come to visit me. I asked her if she knew anyone who would help me interpret the Big Book of Alcoholics Anonymous.

She sent a very kind and generous man named Pete who would come to visit me every two weeks to help me through the Steps. I am forever indebted to this man. This is where I got the notion that recovery is a program *of taking action* and *doing the work*.

By the time I was released in July the next year, I had worked through most of my Steps, One through Nine. On July 11, 1990, my father and cousin came to pick me up.

I met with my sponsor later that day. He took me to a meeting in Beverly Hills that evening— the Roxbury Men's Stag meeting. There I took a cake for my first year of sobriety. I didn't realize I felt nervous but as it turned out I could hardly speak at the podium, I was so filled with emotion.

Susanville correctional facility. 1987. Looking bad ass. Trying to survive one day at a time.

My nephew Michael was with me and I remember him asking me, "Uncle David, aren't you afraid to go in front of all these people?" I responded, "Afraid? I just got out of prison, this is nothing." But I was physically shaking when I got to the podium. All I could say was, "My name is David and I'm an alcoholic. Thank you for my sobriety."

The next day my sponsor drove me to Santa Barbara to check in with the parole department and to drop me off at a sober living facility.

The parole department wasn't very happy to see me. The way the parole system works is, whatever county you last got busted in, that is where you get paroled. They call it the "County of Commitment."

My last county had been Fresno, California and there was no way I wanted to go back. There was nothing there for me. Two years earlier, when I had tried to get sober there, I had been arrested for armed robbery. I was in Fresno to try to kick heroin at my Armenian grandmother's house, (I know what you're thinking: that's pretty gangster, Dave, your *grandmother's* house?). I did end up actually kicking heroin at the time, and then even getting a job. But I was drinking a little bit and smoking weed. That led to the crazy idea, or, should I say, the insane idea: "Maybe I should do a little coke." Cut to the chase: the coke turned into heroin, the heroin turned into a habit, and the habit turned into robberies on the regular. That is how I'd ended my sojourn in Fresno and I was not going back.

If you want to change your parole "County of Commitment," you have to manipulate the system. I wanted to go to Santa Barbara because that is where my ex-girlfriend lived. But they want you to have a place to live, a reason to go to that county (i.e. job, family, recovery), and you have to make a formal request to the parole department to change your County of Commitment. My dad helped me to find a recovery home and my ex-girlfriend wrote a letter. After all was said and done, I was approved for parole in Santa Barbara County.

As I said, they weren't happy to see me. I was sitting in the parole supervisor's office; he called me everything in the book. He said, "I have no idea how you were allowed to come to *my* county. You're a piece-of-shit, armed-robbery dope fiend who we do not want here in Santa Barbara. But for some reason, the fucking state of California agreed to let you come to my county. You're the scum of the earth. If you so much as fart in the wrong direction I'm going to bury you in the system. You'll never get out to see the light of day again."

He asked me, "What do you have to say for yourself?" I said, "Well sir, I have a year of sobriety through the 12 Steps." His response was, "12 Steps, 24 Steps, 48 Steps, I do not give a shit what you do, I do not believe you. I think you're laying in the cut. Now get the fuck out of my office."

I left his office, got into my sponsor's car and my sponsor said, "How'd it go?" I looked at him and said, "I think it went pretty well." Haha!

I checked into sober living. At this point, I had $600 to my name. I didn't really have a trade—before, I had sold drugs, played music, and surfed. Eventually though, I was offered a job working for a sober living home. While working there, I enrolled in Santa Barbara City College without knowing what I would do. I ended up studying psychology. I discovered that I was really interested in how people, the brain, human behavior works. I was especially fascinated with Carl Jung.

As I worked more with newly sober alcoholics and addicts, it seemed they could relate to my approach to the program. I was never judgmental and would not berate anyone; I never have and I never will. A lot of them were new to any "design for living" (recovery program). They'd been living a life of addiction. Most were not used to working with another person in recovery, or doing self-appraisals, or looking at things completely differently than how they had before. I hadn't either. I could remember so vividly when I was where they were.

When I take someone through the Steps, I primarily use the Big Book of AA. The book was written in 1939 with a strong slant towards Christianity. So, when I would talk with the newbies about a higher power, I would not really talk about God in a traditional sense. I stressed a "power greater than ourselves." I talked about what happens in the program, the feeling we get when we are in a group of people—synergy—and synchronicities start to occur; the sense of interconnectedness that happens at a meeting or when working one-on-one with another addict/alcoholic. The people I worked with seemed to connect with that, and also with the idea that it was all about going through the process, and trusting this process.

I was sponsoring a lot of men and counseling people in the sober living facility. My life got better and better. I got married in 1993 and left the sober living home. Subsequently, I got a job at the Klein Bottle youth program in town, which dealt with high-risk youth and drug addiction. There I studied brain chemistry, domestic violence prevention, and how to write treatment plans. This really honed my skills as a lay therapist. I combined my experience in working with 12-Step programs with my background training in psychology. I worked at the Klein Bottle youth program for three years.

In early 1996, the executive director of Newhouse, a sober living facility in Santa Barbara, Bill McCormick, told me about a job opening in the County of Santa Barbara. The job was to design and implement a treatment program for the Santa Barbara County Jail for inmates incarcerated for drug and alcohol-related crimes. I told him I could never work there because of my criminal history. Bill encouraged me to apply for the job anyway. Reluctantly, I turned in my application on February 14, 1996, thinking that my history made this unattainable. I am indebted to Bill for his belief in me when I didn't even believe in myself.

During the interview process, I met the jail's Chief, John Dafoe, who had written the concept paper for this program with Dr. Peter Fransu. Mr. Dafoe invited me into his office and asked me to tell him my entire story. An hour or so later, he knew *everything* about me, I didn't hold back.

I knew I was competing with highly educated people for the job, who were much more qualified than I was academically. There were PhD's as well as MFT's. But when I left his office that day, I felt understood at a fundamental level and uplifted that my perceived lack of qualifications hadn't held me back. I was also amazed that my misadventures into addiction had prepared me for something bigger.

The interview process included an extensive background vetting process. As a part of it, you must list any infractions, crimes, drug use, even school suspensions. This was a very thorough and long process. In the policy and procedure manual of the Santa Barbara Police Department, it says that if you've been convicted of a felony, you cannot work there.

I was sent over to process my paperwork and take a lie-detector test. The detective I met with hadn't been briefed on me and was totally shocked that I had even made it this far in the hiring process. After looking over my paperwork, he said that we could not go forward with this so he did not administer the lie-detector test. When I called the Chief the next day and told him what had happened, he was furious. The rule did not apply to the position I was interviewing for! In the end, I never did take the lie-detector test. But after a very long and tedious process, I got the call offering me the position, which I happily accepted!

I would not have believed it possible just a few short years before. Events and people seemed to align for me—this is how I know the power of synchronicity. If I had to guess why they chose me over all the other candidates who were more educated than I was, it would be because John and Peter knew they needed someone like me who could relate to the other inmates on the same level. I had enough experience clinically, plus, I understood the structure and design of a program. I was hired in November 1996. They gave me a month to write the program, though I'd never written a program before, and have it operational before Christmas.

I threw myself into the task. I was granted twelve beds on the honor farm, a lower custody facility in the county jail. When I sat down to write the program I thought: what would I want if I had to go to a program *anywhere*, not just in the county jail? I implemented individual counseling, group therapy, 12-Step work, processing group, relapse prevention, and educational groups. Rather progressively at the time, we also included yoga and meditation. This is one of my greatest achievements in life, as I see it. I worked there for five years. When I left the county jail, we had 83 beds both for men and women. We had curbed the recidivism rate from 70 percent to 37 percent for individuals who completed the program.

After leaving the Sheriff's Treatment Program, my then-wife and I moved to San Luis Obispo County, where I continued to volunteer for the drug court program as well as run groups in the County Jail. I also kept going to meetings and building a network in the sober community. At one point, I calculated approximately how many newly clean-and-sober alcoholic and addict individuals I had been in contact with during those years. The number was 40,000.

Throughout my journey in recovery and my work with others on that journey, I knew I didn't have to name God as my higher power. I continued to observe that a strictly religious approach made some people hesitate and turned off others. The focus on the energy in a group of people who had the same common goal—

synergy—plus the practical application of the Steps, is what got good results. It was certainly true for me and I saw it work for the addicts I helped, too.

I know I say it all the time, but: *Let us not overthink this. Do the work*: Steps, meetings, service work, helping others. By doing this, by following a set of principles, I shifted the energy in my life from negative to positive. That shift lifted my obsession with alcohol and drugs. My life got better and so will yours.

Using makes your life a very dark, negative energy field. I should have been dead ten times over from the ODs, fights, stabbing, prison riots… the list can go on. When I was an active addict, I was always good at placing the blame on others and would never look at my own behaviors and how I needed to change. I always placed my anger and resentment on someone else, never myself. I didn't know that I needed to look at how *I* could change, not how *the world* could change. Now I live in a positive energy field where I accept what's happening in my life. I take responsibility and do not blame others for my situation. I do not feel the need to defend my point-of-view or force anyone to believe my way of life. In fact, it is like I'm living a whole other life.

What I'm telling you is this: the power of love can overcome anything. It is what kept me alive. I truly believe that. And it is what has brought me here to share this story with you.

One of the greatest things in the Big Book of AA is the Appendix on Spiritual Experience on page 569. I've included it here for you to explore:

"The terms "spiritual experience" and "spiritual awakening" are used many times in this book which, upon careful reading, show that the personality change sufficient to bring about recovery from alcoholism has manifested itself among us in many different forms.

"Yet it is true that our first printing gave many readers the impression that these personality changes, or religious experiences, must be in the nature of sudden and spectacular upheavals. Happily, for everyone, this conclusion is erroneous. In the first few chapters, a number of sudden revolutionary changes are described. Though it was not our intention to create such an impression, many alcoholics have nevertheless concluded that in order to recover they must acquire an immediate and overwhelming "God-consciousness" followed at once by a vast change in feeling and outlook.

"Among our rapidly growing membership of thousands of alcoholics such transformations, though frequent, are by no means the rule. Most of our experiences are what the psychologist William James calls the "educational variety" because they develop slowly over a period of time. Quite often friends of the newcomer are aware of the difference long before he is himself. He finally realizes that he has undergone a profound alteration in his reaction to life; that such a change could hardly have been brought about by himself alone. What often takes place in a few months could seldom have been accomplished by years of self-discipline. With few exceptions, our members find that they have tapped an unsuspected inner resource which they presently identify with their own conception of a Power greater than themselves.

"Most of us think this awareness of a Power greater than ourselves is the essence of spiritual experience. Our more religious members call it "God-consciousness."

"Most emphatically we wish to say that any alcoholic capable of honestly facing his problems in the light of our experience can recover, provided he does not close his mind to all spiritual concepts. He can only be defeated by an attitude of intolerance or belligerent denial.

"We find that no one need have difficulty with the spirituality of the program. Willingness, honesty, and open-mindedness are the essentials of recovery. But these are indispensable."

I like this quote, too, attributed in the Big Book to the English philosopher Herbert Spencer:

"There is a principle which is a bar against all information, which is proof against all arguments and which cannot fail to keep a person in everlasting ignorance. That principle is contempt prior to investigation."

Are you ready to take the Steps?

Trust the Process

Step 1: Acceptance
Step 2: Hope
Step 3: Commitment

CHAPTER 3
Trust the Process

———

ACCEPTANCE, HOPE, COMMITMENT

In the next few chapters, I am going to make the 12 Steps as simple and accessible as possible for you by breaking them down into three different parts. The first part is comprised of Steps 1 through 3, the second part is Steps 4 through 9, and the third part is Steps 10 through 12. This is a program of action, so let's get started!

Step 1

"We admitted we were powerless over alcohol/addiction—that our lives had become unmanageable."

Step One is the only Step we have to do 100% to be able to continue with the rest of the 12-Steps program.

And that is, *abstain from drugs and alcohol.*

It is simply much better working with all the steps if you are abstinent. But, yes, I have worked with people who are still using, from Suboxone to marijuana maintenance; when that's the case, my role is to support and help them bridge from their using to living clean and sober. I would encourage everyone reading this to work through the steps, talk with other addicts, find meetings that are appropriate for your recovery, do the meditations, and take the appropriate actions for you. No matter where you are in your recovery. If you are struggling with abstaining, no judgment here; just keep working the Steps to find your way to full abstinence.

We break down Step One into two parts, the first being that we admit we are powerless over alcohol/addiction. This sense of powerlessness is where I believe an alcoholic/addict has a chemical imbalance, or their chemistry is simply different from a normal drinker. We spoke about this in the Disease Model in Chapter Two, the idea that we lack an internal thermostat to tell us when we have reached our limit with alcohol. Alcoholics seemingly have no limit. So, once we start drinking we trigger the "allergy" which then, in turn, triggers the obsession. We've lost the ability to enjoy and control our drinking. All the research shows that alcoholism is a treatable disease but the allergy itself, or the chemical imbalance, does not go away *ever*. In other words, if a person is sober for an extended period of time and then they start drinking again, they trigger the allergy and will be right back where they left off.

The allergy can only be triggered when we take a drug or drink alcohol. It's the strangest phenomenon that the chemical imbalance or allergy remains, but I've seen this over and over again. People who get away from the program tend to start to believe that having now tasted it, they can control and enjoy their drinking or drugging. Nope! If you have this allergy, you might be able to drink again somewhat normally for a short period of time, but how long that time lasts is unknowable. Know this, though: it will end and you will be powerless over alcohol again, your life unmanageable and back to Step One.

Case in point: I know someone who had nine years of sobriety and decided he no longer needed the program because everything was good with his life, work and relationships. He stopped going to meetings and working the Steps. Then the insane thought came back into his head: "I think I can drink normally now." One night, he was out to dinner with a group of friends and decided to have a couple of beers. Nothing happened. He tried this experiment every couple of weeks and still, nothing severe happened. Four months later, he was on a one-month cocaine, pill and alcohol run and he almost died. He called me from the county jail asking for help.

Let us talk about admitting to being powerless. If an individual does not believe they are powerless over alcohol or drugs, there's no need to go on with the 12 Steps. This is not about modifying your drinking, this is complete abstinence and implementing a whole new design for living. It is my experience that if you remain 100 percent abstinent, you have the best chance of recovery. I encourage you to stay with the process. They say you have to admit to your innermost self that you *are* an alcoholic or simply powerless over alcohol. Only then can you allow the 12-Step program to help you change behaviors and live by a new set of principles.

We have to stop the battle that goes on in the mind. Step One is about actively surrendering that notion or question that maybe we can control our disease. We can't. Period.

When we say we are powerless over our addiction, that is what we mean. We're not necessarily powerless over everything in our lives—we may manage to stay afloat with work or money or relationships, even though we're sick—but we are powerless over the effect of the chemicals we put into our bodies. That's what happens with this particular imbalance or allergy. So, we must actively surrender to this truth on a daily basis. It's an ongoing process for as long as you wish to live sober.

Staying sober is about our relationship with drugs and alcohol, nothing more, nothing less. This isn't about attacking drugs and alcohol themselves, they are not bad or good on their own. It's all about our relationship with them and how they affect us physically. I think some other programs misinterpret what the meaning of powerlessness is in relation to alcoholism/addiction. It's not about a lack of willpower or resolve to stop drinking or drugging. It's about our brain chemistry.

As we learned in Chapter Two, our brain chemistry shifts when we use. Depleting our endorphins and dopamine sends us into a dysphoric state. Alcohol and drugs mimic the effects of dopamine and endorphins that our bodies naturally make in the brain. When we do not get them, we become restless, irritable and discontent.

If you doubt this, or have reservations or you think that someday in your life you'll be able to drink again and not lose control, just know that this has not been my experience or the experience of the thousands of people with whom I have worked. You must get to the point where you admit drugs and alcohol have stopped working for you in your life. If we can get past our reluctance or disbelief that it renders us powerless, and admit to our innermost selves that we *are* powerless over drugs and alcohol, we have made a good beginning.

The second part of Step One says, "My life has become unmanageable." I believe the unmanageability part of the disease is not only that we can't control our using, it's what happens in your entire life while you're under the influence of drugs or alcohol. Alcoholics and addicts lose jobs, have relationship issues, undergo marital problems, go to jail, go to rehab, and develop serious health problems. When we stop drinking and start working a program, all the same things that used to trigger us, such as fear, anxiety, upset, drama, relationships, you name it, can no longer be assuaged with the very substances that destroy our lives.

For many of us, taking drugs or alcohol used to be the only way we knew how to deal with our emotions and problems. That is how we've been programmed, particularly when you've grown up in a family with alcoholics. The 12-Step program, our new design for living, helps us deal with these issues, without going back to our former ways of being.

I remember someone once telling me that "when you get sober you're going to *feel* a lot more." What I found was that yes, I felt intensely, but there were times when I didn't feel very good. What he *meant* is that *all* your feelings will intensify. I had a lot of feelings I couldn't handle, feelings that I didn't know what to do with. For example, I'd be in a social situation, out to coffee after a meeting and I would start to feel overwhelmed. Sometimes I would just leave. This is what really reminded me that drinking and using are just a symptom of my alcoholism. And now I was dealing with life on life's terms. I needed a program not only to get sober but to help me deal with my life sober. The 12 Steps taught me how to deal with emotions and feelings that were uncomfortable.

I think a better way to explain this is, think about if you have not eaten for a day, how would you feel? Hungry, tired, anxious, lightheaded—your body needs food. Let us take it to the next level, you have not eaten in two days. How do you feel? *Really* hungry, tired, and weak! Three days after no food, how do you feel? Desperate, weak, angry, irritable… you would do anything for food at this point… even compromise your principles as a human being. It's the same with drugs and alcohol. When your body is not getting what it needs, massive cravings overtake you.

Dictionary.com defines obsession as "the domination of one's thoughts or feelings by a persistent idea, image, desire, etc." In other words, you're trying *not* to use or drink, but the thought to do it comes into your brain and you cannot stop fixating on the thought or idea. Even though you *know* you should not drink or use drugs, you end up driving right to the liquor store or to the connection. It's nothing else than your brain saying, "I need the stuff." You're depleted of dopamine and endorphins and your brain is yelling, "Give it to me!" You're in a state of extreme dysphoria. That state happens with everyone dealing with this disease. The fact is that when your brain is in a dysphoric state, the obsession can creep in at any time. The good news is that if you don't act on this but instead talk to someone about it, *it will pass.*

What does it mean to be ready for Step One, fully realizing you are powerless over alcohol? One day, I was at a meeting at the Alano Club in Santa Barbara, a home of regular 12-Step meetings. After the meeting, a young man came up to me and said, "I do not know what to do. I want to get loaded and drink right now!"

He was reaching out to me but I didn't want to deal with it at that time. I had a busy day planned and it was inconvenient. I turned to him and said, "Hang in there, man." He responded to me, "What do you mean, 'hang in there?' I want to get loaded right now!" Then I said, "Just let go."

"That makes absolutely no fucking sense," he said. "What kind of weird arithmetic is that? You tell me to hang in there and then say let go?!"

He was a perfect picture of obsession—this young man wanted to drink and use right then and there. He could not get the thought of it out of his mind. He did the right thing by coming to a meeting, yet, it would not subside. I knew at that point, even though it was inconvenient for me, that this guy needed a distraction. So, I told him he could ride along with me and we spent the afternoon together running my errands. All I know is, he didn't drink or use when he was with me; he said the obsession was gone. I dropped him off later at a meeting.

I needed to be there for him. This is what the program is all about; this is another example of synergy. The interaction or cooperation of two or more beings to produce a combined effect greater than the sum of their separate parts. One alcoholic helping another.

Think about it, if you stopped drinking and you felt great, and it was no problem to stay sober, why would you need the program?

Again, we're looking for a design for living to relieve us of the obsession to use. The allergy does not come into play unless you drink or use drugs again, remember that. When I got sober, I made a decision to do whatever it took to change my life from the way I was living. I didn't just sit there and wait for something to happen. I took the appropriate action and I didn't question it when I was going through the process. I just did it. I trusted the process. I got a result. I'll say it again, "*You cannot think your way into the right action, you need to act your way into the right thinking.*"

Think about how many times you've tried to control your drinking or manage the number of substances you take. *It does not work.* Many times, I have heard people say, "I tried just smoking pot and drinking beer," or "I am only doing hard drugs on the weekends." That never works! Invariably, they end up going back to their drug of choice and using on a daily basis. I've had people tell me, "I never really had a problem with alcohol, my problem is methamphetamine." What is that person really telling me? That he/she is going to drink again, and when they drink again, they will end up back on methamphetamine. It happens time and time again.

No matter which way we try to slice it, we are powerless over alcohol or drugs and denial means we always end up back in the same position. If you're lucky enough to be exploring recovery, even just by reading this book, then you're in a position to change your life. Once you're off the drugs and alcohol you have a choice. That is where all your other healthy choices begin. Let us take the journey together.

I think a lot of us in recovery, myself included, took a long time to really know that we could not drink safely or use drugs without consequence. For a long time, I thought that if I just left the hard stuff alone, everything would be fine. It took countless times with disastrous consequences to prove that I cannot drink or use safely.

We are powerless over drugs and alcohol. That's why this is a program of complete abstinence from drugs and alcohol. We need

complete surrender and we need to stop fighting—or bargaining—
with ourselves about whether we can drink or not. We can't. In this
battle, we must surrender to be liberated.

It took me a long time to accept this and abstain from drugs
and alcohol. My turning point came, in part, because other people
planted the seeds in me. It still took me a year after getting arrested
and going back to prison for the last time before I could abstain.

The first time I tried seriously to free myself from addiction,
I was living in Fresno, California at my grandmother's house.
Fresno is 110 degrees in the summer and freezing in the winter.
I'd been in Los Angeles but my cousin convinced me to leave. I
was on parole and on the verge of getting in a lot of trouble by
committing some heinous crime like bank robbery. It was late
spring; I had been strung-out on heroin already for weeks and
needed a place to go to kick. I was in a bad place in my life where
I knew I needed to change but couldn't seem to do it. I felt very
alone at that time. I was thirty-two but felt like I was one million
years old and had lived twenty lifetimes. I didn't know who I
was or what I was doing. Feeling desperate, I headed to Fresno.
When I arrived, the weather was just getting hot. I was committed
to getting off heroin, so I lay on my grandmother's couch sweating
it out, my stomach in knots, throwing up nothing after ten times of
barfing and dry heaves. The leg cramps were so bad that I felt like
someone was sticking a knife in my leg all the way to the marrow
of my bones. It is said that if you can get through the first five days
of an opiate kick then the rest is all about trying to get some sleep.
I started to feel okay after about the tenth day, and my parole was
finally transferred from L.A. to Fresno. My cousin set me up to get a
job at Gallo wine. They were interviewing people to be hired for the
crush, a seasonal job that started mid-July and ended early in October.
In retrospect, what was I thinking, working for a company that
produced alcohol? But my cousin had a friend who was a higher-up

there and he let me know to come in clean because they would drug-test me when I interviewed. I was completely off drugs at the time. It's a telling reflection of society at that time—1988—that they interviewed 1,000 people for 100 jobs and 700 of them failed the drug test. Out of the remaining 300 job candidates, I got one of the hundred jobs.

I started out on the graveyard shift. The heat in Fresno was so intense that it was even still warm at night. I remember how it smelled at the winery; there was a weird kind of toxic, chemical smell mingling with fermenting grapes. The old-timers would always find a good way to set you up for a laugh. One time I was cleaning one of the 600,000-gallon tanks there. I had forgotten the warning when you open the tank: step aside or the fermenting gas will knock you out! When I opened one of the doors, the next thing I remember is waking up, passed out on the ground. One of the old-timers was laughing. He asked me, "Did your balls get warm before you passed out?" It was a good job and I thought I had my addiction licked. I was working seven days a week. After work, I would go home and help my grandma cook and play backgammon. I never socialized with any of my fellow workers or anyone else. I was making a little bit of money and giving my grandmother some. I thought that's all I had to do. I had not treated my alcoholism/addiction, all I did was not use drugs and alcohol. I believe if you are an alcoholic that abstaining without a program only lasts so long. I had done well at my job, made the union and was scheduled to come back and work the next season. They were very pleased with my work; I was now part of the crew. I knew how to work the winery. I was feeling good, generally. So good that one day after my shift, I had an insane idea that I would get a little coke—not heroin—a little coke couldn't hurt, right? But I had no idea where to go to score. I was not from Fresno, I had no other connections besides my grandmother there and didn't know anyone else. I knew, though, that if I went to where the hookers hung out, there was a good possibility that I could score. I also thought if I went to the methadone clinic that I might be able to connect. I asked some random person where the hookers hung out. He told me a street but it turned out to be the wrong avenue. It was very hot that day, the air felt heavy, it was overcast and the smell of the San Joaquin Valley, the chemicals in the air, seemed to permeate your clothes. There was nobody on the street he'd suggested. I walked around and finally happened upon an area where people were walking the streets and hustling. I saw what I thought could possibly be someone who I could connect with and, sure enough, I was able to score a gram of coke. It lasted me a few days which was completely amazing because in the past, when I was in my addiction, it would only have lasted two shots. That first week's experiment went so well, that I thought I should get just a little bit of heroin and shoot a speedball. That couldn't hurt. I scored a gram of heroin and a gram of coke. Putting it in the spoon and heating it up with matches almost made me feel like I was home again. Watching that brown liquid start to boil, the smell that would almost make you throw up, but it was the most welcoming, loving, healing smell that you could ever imagine. Filling the syringe, knowing that there was no turning back, puncturing the vein, drawing back on the needle, watching the blood mix with the loving brown heroin. Injecting heroin into my veins was a feeling like no other feeling. Every pain, emotional, spiritual, physical had left my body and I knew I was home. I'm not sure if I even thought, hey, I should try to keep this under control, because now I felt so comforted.

At the same time, I knew I had fucked up and there was no turning back. I knew I would end up in a bad place; it was over. I was able to keep my job because I did not get a habit for a couple of weeks. But three weeks later, I wasn't showing up for work. The job was pretty much over for the crush by then anyway. Bailing on the last few weeks, I had blown my chances of ever coming back there.

By this time, I had about a gram-a-day habit. The place I was scoring drugs was in the ghetto on Fresno's West Side. I had met a

Latina girl who was turning tricks and had a pretty big habit. She was amazingly beautiful, but the streets were taking a toll on her. She wasn't more than twenty-seven years-old; I was thirty-two. Her hair was jet black, her skin was paler than it should have been, and she probably had some of the worst tracks I've ever seen. I could look in her eyes and see there was nothing there. Heroin addicts are so shut down that you're just going through the motions of life without emotion, let alone any kind of spirituality. Heroin is a very self-centered drug. For some reason, she fell for me, or she just knew I was easily manipulated to help her commit crimes. We started working together doing robberies. I didn't care what I was sinking into because for some reason I had a strong connection with her. And heroin makes you not care about anything else. There was no turning back at this point. She had a studio close to the railroad tracks on the West Side. It was in an old apartment building. Broken-down cars slouched in the parking lot. I could always hear people screaming and fighting. I remember hearing someone laughing so loudly there that it almost felt out of place. We would fix dope, laugh, and make love in that shitty little apartment. It was like time stood still; for a moment, we had everything. There was nothing more that we needed in that moment.

This girl had more heart than any guy I've ever met. Heart, in prison terms, means that a person just does not care at all and will go to any lengths to get what they want, even if it means killing a cop. Why she talked me into the things that she talked me into, I have no idea. I was so messed up. We had two guns; one was a .38 that didn't work, the other was a 9 mm. We probably did ten robberies together. She was way more of a criminal at heart than I was, in the sense that she kind of had a plan and I never did.

One of the robberies scared me more than the others. She knew of a deli where we could probably get $1,500. She knew where the owner kept the money in the safe, behind the cartons of cigarettes. I walked in first, put a gun in his face and told him to give me all the money or I'd blow his face off. My heart was racing. I was sweating like a racehorse. She stood behind me with the broken .38 caliber pistol. The man didn't move. I believe he was Armenian, like me. Looking at him, it could have been either of us on the other side of the gun. He kept repeating, "I work hard for my money." I was in such a panic; I kept yelling at him to give me the fucking money. He grabbed a knife and started walking toward me. The last thing I wanted to do was shoot anybody. Thankfully, his wife saved us—she walked out from the back and said, "Give him the money." She was crying. I think we got $1,150. I'll never forget the smell of that store. It was almost like everything was stale and they had been cooking some awful food in the back. On our way home we ordered Chinese takeout, scored three grams of heroin, a couple grams of cocaine, and headed back to her flat. I sat in my boxers, she in her underwear; we were shooting dope all night. We were both in paradise. I knew then that I was completely engulfed emotionally with this girl. The next day we had enough dope to get us through the next twenty-four hours. She said she had to leave, that she had a John that paid her pretty well. She went out the following night. She kissed me slowly on the lips, looked in my eyes like she was looking into my soul, and I knew in that moment that she loved me. She told me she would see me in the morning. We parted and I was sure I would see her again. I needed to see her again. The next morning, she didn't come home and I was almost out of dope. I went, scored, and thought it would be a good idea to check on my grandmother, who I hadn't seen for a couple weeks. I sat with my grandmother, who had no idea what was going on. I told her that I had been staying with friends for a couple of weeks. (I had been checking in with her so she hadn't been worried.) I stayed at my grandmother's for a couple of days. Then I went back to my girlfriend's flat. No one was around. It looked exactly the same as when I left three days earlier. Had she come home? I checked with the people that I knew on the streets who knew her, they had not seen her. I was worried about her and in the same breath, I was relieved. I hoped that she was okay, and that she had found some peace. I never saw her again in my life. There's always a place in my heart for her. Being shut down, there was still a part of me that longed to be loved and to give love. It was so dysfunctional and in the same breath, comforting. We were two kids lost in the world of drugs and crime, lost in the game.

Now without my partner in crime, I still thought it best to do a couple more robberies. I was so desperate for drugs that I robbed a gas station from which I had bought cigarettes the day before. It was a drive-through and I think I had my grandmother with me when I bought the cigarettes.

I didn't score much money from that robbery, maybe only $250, which was gone within a day or so. I used some of the money to get on methadone at the clinic downtown. I was on the run from my parole officer, so I left town for two weeks to stay with an ex-girlfriend in Santa Maria. When I came back to my grandmother's house, she told me that the parole department had been looking for me. So, I went downtown and stayed with one of my drug connections for a few days. I knew I was in a bad place again but I still couldn't admit why: that *I was powerless over my disease.*

After about a week, I called my grandmother. She reported that a friend of mine named James had called and wanted to see me. He was coming through town on his way back East. James was a good friend of mine who had been a severe heroin addict. He'd gotten clean a few years before. He was an amazing poet and songwriter, as well as an artist. He always encouraged me to write, sing, play music, and talk about my life. We would sit and smoke cigarettes back in the day and shoot heroin when times were good. I called him back and, sure enough, he was coming through town in a couple of days, and would like to see me. I didn't want to meet James at my grandmother's house and obviously not at the connection's. We met downtown at a liquor store near the methadone clinic. It was getting cold at the time, I was out of money, I was out of hustle, I was pretty pathetic. The streets were dirty. Toxic wind from the San Joaquin Valley blew the trash in the gutters. I had been up all night shooting coke and heroin. My veins were torn up, there was dried blood on my shirt. I was not in good shape. When James showed up he was a breath of fresh air. I'd never seen him look so good. His eyes were clear, his skin was glowing. He looked like he had found some peace. He gave me a big hug and kissed my forehead. He knew I was dying inside. He was like a big brother to me. I felt safe around him.

I owed $40 at the methadone clinic and they wouldn't dose me without me paying my bill. So, one of the first things I asked James was if he could loan me $40. He looked at me, not with disgust. He was a recovering addict. He knew how I felt, he had been in the same place several times during his addiction. James looked at me and only wanted me to get better. He was coming from a place of love and compassion and, I'm sure, a lot of sadness. He said he would give me the money, But before he did, he looked me straight in the eye and said he wanted to tell me something. He said he loved me and didn't want to see me die. He also said something to me that I have never forgotten to this day, "You're killing yourself, brother. This is your life, not the parole department's, not your grandmother's, not your girlfriend's, not anyone's. This is *your* life, and I want you to live." He had tears in his eyes. So did I. I loved him and I knew he loved me. We were two junkies, one still practicing and one that had made it to the other side. What he said was a wakeup call to me that was part of the beginning of my new life. It felt like turning a corner. Though my recovery didn't start for another year or so, what James said had an effect on me that hasn't left me to this day. He had admitted he was powerless over his addiction and his life had become unmanageable. He had started his recovery with Step One and in time so would I.

The next couple of weeks were pretty tough. I was done. Done running, done trying to get clean, done trying to do the right thing. I knew I was going back to the penitentiary but I didn't know when or how soon. It was just a matter of time. I had been staying down at the connection's place on the West Side. I decided to go back to my grandmother's house. I was there only two days; I wanted to kick but I was still doing anything it took to get a little bit of heroin, and also taking some Valiums and codeines to help me get through the day.

Now I was wanted for parole violation as well as new robberies. The day of reckoning came only two days after I went back to my grandmother's house. It was early, about 7 a.m. I was standing in front of the kitchen sink, which had a window that looked out onto the front lawn. This was a working-class neighborhood, good people, kids playing in the front yards, dogs barking, people getting ready for the workday. Looking out the window, I saw two men coming up the walkway to the front door. They were wearing suits. I knew who they were and I knew why they were coming. Thoughts raced through my mind: maybe I should run, maybe I should start jumping fences in the backyard, maybe I should try to lie and convince them that I'm not who they think I am. But drugs had stolen my capacity to feel, to care. It's the weirdest feeling when you don't give a shit and you're just happy that the game is coming to an end. I wasn't going to be arrested, I was going to be *rescued*. I remembered the words my friend James had said to me, "*This is your life, brother, no one else's.*"

I answered the door and they asked me to step outside immediately, where they handcuffed me and put me face down on the grass. My grandmother was screaming, crying, "He's a good boy! What are you doing? Leave him alone!" By that time there were three squad cars, plus the parole department, parked in front of the house. It was over. Sitting in the back of the undercover agent's car on my way to county jail, the handcuffs were digging into my skin. I remember the stench of bad air freshener in the car. The detectives issued threats as they hauled me to jail; when they talked, I could hear them but it was surreal, it was just background noise. Looking out the car window, I could see that it was cold outside. People were going to work, living normal lives. I watched them knowing that I was looking at my last views of freedom, on my way back to the penitentiary.

When I was booked into the Fresno County Jail I felt a sense of relief. Being a junkie is a full-time job; once you're addicted it's not about getting loaded anymore, it's about getting to the point where you at least feel some sort of relief. I was already feeling pretty sick, knowing that I was going to have to kick my habit and what that involved. It wasn't a bad habit, or so I thought, only about a gram a day. I had kicked heroin in jail before. It's no fun but it's actually a little easier than trying to do it on the street because you don't have a lot of options around you to get dope. Don't get me wrong, there's dope in prison and jail but it's just not as easy to access as it is on the streets.

They took me into a room to get processed. Two detectives sat there waiting for me. I knew this game oh so well; I'd been playing it since I was 13. Good cop, bad cop. They try to get you to roll on someone. They try to frighten you with going to prison for the rest your life. It's all a bunch of bullshit and I knew that. When they went through the routine, it was like background noise to me. I sat there thinking about why my life had gotten to this point. What was going to happen to me? Jail has a bizarre look and feel, it's almost like being underground. Not a lot of sunlight. It has this disgusting smell of cleaning supplies on top of burnt coffee, on top of urine and shit.

At one point, one of the detectives yelled at me and said, "Are you listening to me, tough guy? You're going to prison for a long time. You better start talking!"

He stormed out of the room and left me with the other detective. This is part of the theatrical game that they play, but for some reason it was different this time. This detective, a family man in his mid-forties, wanting to do the right thing for his community, turned his chair around backwards and sat right in front of me. He asked me how I was doing. Then, he proceeded to tell me that they knew I did the robberies, and they also believed that I had robbed fourteen Kentucky Fried Chicken restaurants. I thought that was fucking hilarious. Anyway, I let him do his job, I said nothing, pleaded not guilty, and told him that he didn't know what he was talking about, I did nothing. Then there was a twist. It was like he was almost an extension of my friend James, and I went into this euphoric state.

He said, "You are going back to prison. We know we can convict you on one robbery, you've already been identified. But I look at you and for some reason, not sure what it is, but I know that this is not what you're supposed to be doing. This is not you, this whole jail prison bullshit." At that point, he offered me a cigarette and a candy bar. I welcomed both. He said, "You're a heroin addict. I'm a recovering alcoholic. I've been sober for eleven years." He said, "There's a way out of this and someday I picture you with a pick-up truck, family, children, being a productive member of society. For some reason you're different, but you're the same as the rest." He looked me straight in the eye, his eyes welled up, he was fighting back the tears. I was so shut down emotionally that I don't think I could cry at that point. I don't even think I responded. He stood up, went to the door, motioned to one of the correctional officers to take me to my cell and that was it.

I remember what the detective said to me. Remember, he was the enemy in my world. Yet, like James, he came from a place of compassion and genuinely wanting to help. Seeds get planted on the way to our recovery. We never know who the messenger is, or what the messages will be. But I knew this man was coming from a place of true love and compassion for another suffering alcoholic/drug addict. He was carrying the message. I'll never forget him. Sometimes it doesn't even feel real, but a year-and-a-half later to the day I took my last shot of heroin. My friend James, who had carried the first message to me, is no longer with us. He died of complications from hepatitis C. He'd been clean and sober at the time of his death for more than 20 years.

The detective in the Fresno County Jail, whose name I never knew, also carried the message and planted the seed of recovery in me. I am forever grateful and blessed that these two men were in my life. They led me to Step One.

Step 2

"Came to believe that a Power greater than ourselves could restore us to sanity."

I like this Step. Notice that they don't mention the word, "God." Instead, they used, *"a power greater than yourself."*

This is the power I call "synergy," along with the power of working a program. When you ask most people how they would describe a power greater than themselves, nine times out of ten, they answer, "God." Sometimes I hear "nature," "the ocean," or "my spouse." There are some powers larger than us that we simply cannot control. The power of the universe, the power of the tides, the power of the ocean, the power of nature, the power of love. These are all powers greater than ourselves.

Someone told me once that their higher power was a doorknob. I thought to myself, well, that's an interesting analogy. It didn't work for me initially—a doorknob?—but then he went on to explain that, over time, by working the program, that doorknob turned into a door and the door opened and turned into a light. He said the light was love, compassion, and trust. That was what his higher power turned out to be, over a period of time, by working the 12 Steps. He depended on, or better connected with, this form of a higher power that helps him get through his life one day at a time.

A woman told me her higher power was Mother Nature. When she was running, or simply sitting in nature quietly and connecting to the energy of the plants, ocean, trees, and animals, she said she found peace, calm and love. If she focused on the energy in nature, that gave her strength.

It is very personal, wherever you find a power greater than yourself. When I sit in meetings, I feel the power of love. People are there to get help or to give help freely. To me, there is an immense beauty and power in that. When I'm working with another person, helping them understand the 12-Step process, I become empowered. I feel unconditional love and a sense of selflessness. The peace and serenity I feel are like no other drug I've ever taken. And, it's *sustainable*.

In Step 2, we are asked to believe that although we admit we are powerless over our disease in Step 1, there *is* a power that can relieve our alcoholism/addiction. By doing that, we will be restored to sanity. I believe this has a lot to do with faith. What is the definition of faith? Faith is defined as "complete trust or confidence in someone or something." So, it has to do with *reliance*. I believe if you work the Steps and go through the program, you need to find someone you can trust to be by your side. For me, and for many alcoholics and addicts, that person was my sponsor. I just knew if I did what he asked me to do, I would not have to go back to the life I'd been living. I didn't necessarily want what he had, I just trusted in the process and his guidance. What did I have to lose?

Ask yourself, are you willing to believe that following the program will help you with your alcoholism? By "following the program," I mean, following directions from your sponsor, allowing the synergy of the program to flow, doing everything that is asked of you (going to meetings, working the Steps, being honest, living by a set of principles, etc.), allowing others to help you, and practicing honesty, willingness, and open-mindedness. If you are an alcoholic or addict like I was, you know you are out of choices. I was willing to do anything at that point in my life to not go back to drinking and using. All the program asks of you is to believe—or be willing to believe—that a higher power can help restore you to sanity. I ask you, what do you have to lose?

Let us talk first about "sanity." The Step says, "*A power greater than yourself can restore you to sanity.*" My response thirty years ago was, "I do not believe I'm insane! I do not belong in a mental institution!" My sponsor explained it to me like this: After taking Step One fully, admitting you're powerless over alcohol/addiction, you realize that the most insane thing to do in reference to your life, *knowing* that you are an alcoholic/addict and having *admitted* that you are powerless over that substance, would be to drink or use. Make sense?

No one is saying that you're insane or maladjusted to anything else in your life. But knowing that you're an alcoholic or addict means that for you *to drink or drug again would be insane.* I've heard it in meetings (and so will you) that "Insanity is doing the same thing over and over and expecting different results." Especially when it's *continuing to use* despite the same adverse results.

Let us talk specifically about the words sanity and insanity. Sanity is defined as "wholeness of mind" or being able to process a cognitive or rational thought—here we use it in reference to alcohol or drugs. For example, if you put your hand into a fire, it burns. Most likely, if you were not insane, you would not put your hand back into the fire—once is enough. When there are adverse consequences, sane people most likely will not do the same thing over and over and expect something different to happen—or not care when it doesn't.

When I was working in the jail running the sheriff's treatment program, I would see normal people, non-alcoholics or addicts, get arrested for drunk driving or otherwise end up in the drunk tank for being drunk in public. This might happen to them at a party or on New Year's Eve or whatnot. Even non-alcoholics have adverse consequences as a result of drinking too much. The difference between a normal, temperate drinker and an alcoholic/addict is that the normal person will say, "That was an awful experience. I'll never do that again." And nine out of ten times they won't. The alcoholic/addict will say, "Oh, that'll never happen to me again and that wasn't my fault." Or, "Once I start drinking again, I can control the behavior." I cannot tell you how many times an addict has told me they will never do that again. Then they end up drunk (again), or using, and they wind up back in jail, losing their job, having marital and health problems… the list goes on. According to the 12-Step literature, the only way to be relieved of alcoholism and/or addiction is to find a power greater than ourselves and believe in it. We need to have a spiritual awakening. We can do this by connecting to the power of "synergy." You can do this, and you do not have to do it in a religious way.

I once heard it said and it stuck with me: "You cannot start a revolution on a full stomach." There must be the gift of desperation for change to occur because if everything is going well, why would you make a change? The motivation for change comes when we are bankrupt physically, spiritually, and emotionally. And we realize we need to rely on something bigger than us.

I know some of the wealthiest people in the world who are the unhappiest because of this disease. They can have everything materially that the world has to offer, but they feel completely alone. This disease does not discriminate between rich and poor or in any other way. There is no class system in addiction. When we walk into the rooms, we're on an even playing field.

One old-timer in the program whose nickname was Singing Sam used to say, "It does not matter if you're from Park Avenue or the park bench. Or if you come from Yale or jail." In all instances, love overcomes hate and faith overcomes fear.

I want to introduce another concept here. All of us, as sentient (feeling) beings have a Higher Self as well as a Lower Self. I believe that when we are in our active disease, we are connected to our lower self and that we are vibrating at a lower frequency. In the universe, there are high and low vibrations. Positive actions, feelings, and emotions have a higher energetic frequency whereas negative feelings, actions, and emotions have lower vibrational frequencies. Think of all the things that happen during the times of your active addiction: fights, getting in trouble, not thriving at work, compromising our principles or morals, sleeping with someone we normally would not, cheating on our partners, doing outrageous things to get drugs or alcohol that we would never do sober: lying, cheating, or stealing. The higher self would be exemplified, instead, by doing things like helping other people without expecting anything in return, sitting and reading with a child, performing selfless acts for others, helping a newcomer with the Steps, taking someone to a meeting, meditation, yoga and exercise, positive self-talk and being kind to yourself.

Perhaps, the outer circumstances of our lives are seemingly not that bad but internally, we are dying inside. I have worked with people who live an affluent lifestyle where they didn't lose everything. They even had people around them to take care of everything they could possibly need and want, but they still hit rock bottom, not in an alley but at a fancy cocktail party. They were emotionally bankrupt; something needed to change. They needed to connect with a loving power greater than themselves.

Moving into a higher vibrational field, our Higher Self, changes everything. By doing this, we practice different things such as honesty, compassion, trust, joy, forgiveness. A higher vibrational being knows when something is in alignment with it or not. We all have an intuitive sense of what is right and what is wrong. Our higher self can't ignore it.

When I was getting sober, it became starkly clear what was not comfortable in my life anymore. Lying, and cheating no longer worked. They have no place in the life of a sober person working an honest program; that person finds them intolerable. The dichotomy is too great.

Alcoholics who strive to better themselves in sobriety become some of the most hardworking and honest people out there. We've all compromised our principles for a drink or a drug. We aren't judging here, it's simply what happened. The ones who seemingly used to be the most immoral creatures on the planet are now productive members of society contributing to their communities in the most selfless way! They thrive on feeding the homeless and being of service. They cannot give you incorrect change, even by five cents. In the same way, they used to fixate on how to get their needs met or how to get their next fix. Now their minds will not let them disengage if they do something even the slightest bit off their path. They are now vibrating on a higher plane; they are connected to their Higher Self. Life is no longer about them and what they can take from this world, it's about what they can give back. That is what happens when you practice Step Two.

Step 3

"Made a decision to turn our will and our lives over to the care of God, as we understood Him."

This is according to the traditional literature; they use the word God. I simply replace the word with a Higher Power or the program as the Higher Power. *"As we understood Him,"* I interpret as: how I understand this power or synergy. There is a power in going through the rest of the program by taking the appropriate steps and working with a sponsor. There is a *huge* power in that. So, Step Three can be read as, *"Made a decision to turn our will and our lives over to the care of a higher power, as we understood this higher power."*

To me, this Step is really all about committing and dedicating ourselves to the process of the rest of the 12 Steps. Here they're asking us to turn "your will and your life" over to a power greater than yourself. Or in other words, turn your life over to the process of the program. Or the "synergy" of the program. Nothing more, nothing less. When you practice Step Three, you're making a decision to go on.

What is will and what is life? The way I break this down is that human beings do two things and two things only—we think and we act. So, basically, Step Three is asking us to turn our thoughts and our actions over to the care of the program, or if you prefer, a "power greater than yourself." Care is an important word here. You're not just turning your will and your life over to something, you're turning it over to something that is going to take "care" of you. That meant a lot to me. I wasn't just marching down the road; I felt that other people had compassion and love for the process on which I was about to embark. I was taken care of, I was not alone. I had turned my will over to the care of these people with compassion and love.

Another way I looked at it was that I was turning my will and my life over to the care of someone that is an expert in this field. For example, when I take my car in for repairs, I want that person who is working on my car to have professional training as a mechanic. I also want him or her to take care of my car, making repairs carefully and mindfully. So, working Step Three, when I say "professional," I don't mean we're paying a professional to help us along the 12-Step path. (Many of us are also in psychotherapy or other social services apart from our focused program work; here I am talking specifically about the "expertise" of others who work the program.) We are taking direction from someone who knows what they're doing, our sponsor or a program mentor. They are the experts who have a working knowledge of the 12 Steps. Their experience and knowledge helps us and guides us through the process.

To break this Step down further, "will" is defined as active action. When someone writes a last Will and Testament, that is symbolically their last "action" in life, explaining their will—what

Early sobriety. Trying to assimilate back into society
after a long stay in the penitentiary.

they want to happen after they pass. We also think of self-will. What is that? It isn't your willpower, as you might think, it's that we're programmed to do things in a certain way without self-will. Before the program, you did what you wanted to do. Now you have to take direction from someone else or do something that seems contrary to you. It comes down to following the will of the program, following directions and going through with the process of the rest of the Steps. Trust the process! Again, let us not get confused. We're turning our action over to the care of this 12-Step program. This act will help us find a new design for living that deals with our addiction or alcoholism. Some of the "contrary-feeling" actions that you will be taking are going to meetings, making commitments, working with a sponsor, and helping other people. Remember, we're looking to live by a set of principles, to connect with the energy, the synergy, of the program.

It's not just turning over our actions to the care of the program, we must also turn over our thoughts to the program's care, or the care of the power greater than yourself that you choose.

If I was judged by my thoughts, I'd be in big trouble. This is why I love to repeat, "*You cannot think your way into the right action, you need to act your way into the right thinking.*" By doing this over and over, it becomes a working part of your life. For example, you might think, "I'm fine. I don't need to go to a meeting tonight," but you get up and go anyway. You're acting your way into the right thinking. The 12 Steps are a program of *action*, not of *thinking*.

I like to go running. It's a part of my workout practice. There are times when I just don't want to go and I can think of any excuse not to. But I have learned and believe that it is a part of my retraining in the program to push through my excuses and go running anyway. I sit there thinking about how much I don't want do this as I'm putting on my shoes. I think about it as I walk out the door and I think about it as I start running down the street. But, I can tell you this, I always feel better once I'm done with my run. I'm acting my way into the right thinking, plus I get a shit ton of endorphins.

By doing the actions, your thoughts are going to change. You have guidelines to live by, a set of principles to work towards. Remember, these are a set of perfect principles that we'll never *actually* perfect. We will just work *towards* perfection. Someone once told me, "Practice does not make perfect, practice *is* perfect." Remember, do the work, practice the program, live by a set of principles, connect with the synergy. By doing this you will get results.

Though we may be replacing the word "God" with "program" or "higher power" as we do Step Three, I want us to look at some of the wording from Step Three that is in the original Big Book's discussion of this Step:

"This is the how and why of it. First of all, we had to quit playing God. It didn't work. Next, we decided that hereafter in this drama of life, God was going to be our Director. He is the Principal; we are His agents. He is the Father, and we are His children. Most good ideas are simple, and this concept was the keystone of the new and triumphant arch through which we passed to freedom. When we sincerely took such a position, all sorts of remarkable things followed. We had a new Employer. Being all powerful, He provided what we needed, if we kept close to Him and performed His work well. Established on such a footing we became less and less interested in ourselves, our little plans and designs. More and more we became interested in seeing what we could contribute to life. As we felt new power flow in, as we enjoyed peace of mind, as we discovered we could face life successfully, as we became conscious of His presence, we began to lose our fear of today, tomorrow or the hereafter. We were reborn." (From the Big Book of Alcoholics Anonymous, pages 62-63).

In my version of this passage, I replace the word God with "the program."

That passage is followed by a prayer:

"*God, I offer myself to Thee—to build with me and to do with me as Thou wilt. Relieve me of the bondage of self, that I may better do Thy will. Take away my difficulties, that victory over them may bear witness to those I would help of Thy Power, Thy Love, and Thy Way of life. May I do Thy will always!*" (The Big Book of Alcoholics Anonymous, page 63.)

My version of the prayer that made it easier for me to connect with the power of the program and Step Three is as follows:

"*I dedicate myself to the program, to build with me and to do with me as it will. Relieve me of the bondage of self that I may do the program's will. Take away my difficulties, that victory over them will bear witness to those I would help of the power, the love, and the way of life. May I work towards living these principles daily.*"

My version reflects what most people would say if they had to describe the 12-Step program in two words: love and service. The three things that they talked about in the statement from the Big Book above are:

1. Power (synergy)
2. Love (the compassionate service we can give to others)
3. Way of Life (the new principles by which we are living)

Just looking at this makes so much sense. By doing the work and combining those three elements—power, love, and the program's way of life— we're connected to a positive way of living. By doing the work on an ongoing basis, one day at a time, one breath at a time, our life *will* get better. Remember, by shifting the energy, by living by a new set of principles, by not drinking or using, this will happen. Living this way after a period of time will become a working part of your life; your "normal," day-to-day life. If it does not work, then go back to what you were doing! (No. Do not. Trust the process!) You basically have nothing to lose and everything to gain.

Let us continue, shall we?

Cleaning House, Part 1

Step 4: Uncovering
Step 5: Trust
Step 6: Willingness
Step 7: Humility

CHAPTER 4
Cleaning House, Part 1

───

Step 4

"We made a searching and fearless moral inventory of ourselves."

This is the first Step of the key middle six-steps process—Steps Four, Five, Six, Seven, Eight, and Nine—all of which call on you to take action. In this chapter, we'll cover Steps 4-7. If I had to summarize these steps, I'd quote the Japanese writer, Haruki Murakami, who wrote, "Pain is inevitable, suffering is optional."

In Steps 4-7 we tackle the pain. Step Four, writing your inventory, is basically the foundation for working the other five Steps in this sequence. Step Four is really the first action Step. Or, I should say "literal action." Some people would argue with me that the preceding three Steps are also action Steps, in that we *admit* (Step One), we *believe* (Step Two) and we *make a decision* (Step 3).

But here we take the first *physical* action: putting pen to paper. I like to have people write out Step Four in longhand because I believe it is a more therapeutic process than typing it on a computer or phone. When you're writing with a pen or a pencil, you're saying it, you're feeling it, you're hearing it. Your handwriting is uniquely your own and I find that, besides giving you an intense feeling of owning your inventory, the process makes it more engaging. That what I believe, anyway, but do it whatever way works for you. The point is you're doing it.

When I did my first inventory, there were no lights that suddenly came on; I had no epiphanies. I hear many people say that after they wrote their Fourth Step, they felt a huge relief, like a thousand-pound overcoat came off their back.

I can completely appreciate that. For me, I felt I completed a task and that action made me feel like I was truly part of the program. I did something visible and concrete. Do not get me wrong; I really had a strong feeling, and I felt connected to the program or "synergy" of the program from the start. But there is something powerful about Step Four because you have committed yourself to rigorous, honest self-examination and for an alcoholic or addict that can be the breakthrough step to sobriety.

A lot of people tell me that they have a problem with Step Four. I do not think they're having a problem with Step Four, I think that they're actually having a problem with Step Three. The reason I say that is because if you've made a decision as well as a commitment to go forward with the program, knowing you will do it with care and love, there should be no hesitation. If someone says they're having a problem with Step Four, I suggest they go back and look at Step Three to probe whether they have really made a firm decision to turn their will and their life over to the care of the program. Remember, in Step Three we are making a commitment to go forward, that is all. Once you have made that commitment, you *want* to take forward action.

Step Four is the first Step that looks at our patterns of behavior, shortcomings, and character defects. Getting all of this down on paper, we are able to reflect on what is working in our lives and what is not working.

Step Four says we made a "searching and fearless moral inventory." "Moral" is defined as right or wrong behavior. So, it says right there that we're looking for behaviors that once worked for us when we were using or drinking and now we are looking for behaviors that are *no longer working for us* in our new life of sobriety. For example, lying, cheating, or manipulating, all of which we did to sustain our addiction.

Dictionary.com defines an "inventory" as "a complete listing of merchandise or stock on hand, work in progress, raw materials, finished goods on hand, etc., made each year by a business concern." Our inventory is a record of our lives—we are now writing down everything about them. (We'll put it into three categories to make the process easier. I'll break that down shortly.)

The AA literature also uses the word "fearless." We're going into this knowing we're not alone, that we're plugged into an energy that is loving, compassionate and caring. We're looking for a new design for living, so we launch into a course of vigorous action, which many of us have never done before. Before Step Four, I had never written about my own behavior. I had done a lot of journaling describing my various activities, but nothing like this; nothing this personal. This was a retrospective of my life. It really helped. At this point in my thirty years of sobriety, I have now done several inventories and I am living a life that I would have never dreamed of in my old days.

Let us get into it. The Fourth Step is broken down into three parts: **resentments, fears,** and **sexual conduct**. I like to look at the last one as more about how we act in relationships, not just sexual ones. We go through each category and get these all down on paper.

Resentment: what is resentment, really? Bad feelings, hard feelings, indignation, a sense of being treated unfairly, having a resentment toward people, places, or things. In the 12-Step process, the literature states that resentments are our number one self-offender. If we cannot get over these, we will possibly drink or use again. To drink or use again could possibly kill us.

Another way resentments are unhealthy is that they release chemicals in our bodies that compromise our immune system.

The most common one is cortisol or the stress hormone. This is a chemical that your body releases when you have high levels of stress, anger, and hypertension. Think about it. When you get angry or upset, sometimes you get physically ill. That is cortisol being released into your system, which compromises your immune system, which makes you susceptible to diseases that could ultimately kill you— diseases like cancer, heart disease, and hypertension.

When I studied psychology at Santa Barbara City College, I took a class called Physiological Psychology. It was usually pretty boring to me, but I was completely engaged one day when the professor lectured on brain chemistry. He referred to a study that showed that people who harbor stress, anger, hyperactivity, or resentment are more susceptible to all kinds of diseases. You can see the correlation to brain chemistry and know that, as alcoholics, we must get rid of our resentments or they will eventually kill us. Not only will it drive us back to using or drinking, but in the meantime, it could compromise our overall physical health dramatically. Making that connection was an important landmark in my sobriety. I started to care about my health in a new way.

I've found that creating a worksheet helps organize your inventory and makes it more comprehensive. To get started, make four columns on a sheet of paper. In the first column, list all the people, places and things you have resentments about or grudges towards, anyone who has harmed or hurt you up to this point in your life. Just start writing it down. Do nothing in column two until you have completed column one. An easy way to approach it is to start with immediate family, go on to extended family, then friends, ex-relationships, etc. Keep going further out with places and institutions. It could be the institution of marriage or religion, but it could also be the college that flunked you or the parole department that put you back in prison. You know who they are and, chances are, you have held many of your resentments for *years*. Now is the time to own them.

In column two, write down the reason you are resentful or angry at said person or institution. Again, do nothing in column three until you have completed column two. Column three is what parts of your life all these resentments affected. An example of columns one and two would be, "I am resentful at the institution of marriage because it never seems to work out. My parents got a divorce and it affected me deeply." In the third column, how this resentment affected you, you'd write something like, "My parents' divorce caused me to drink and use."

Column four will be the turnaround where you find your part in this.

Referring to column three, generally, we break down the "self" into seven parts affected by our resentments. They are:

- Self-esteem - how I think of myself
- Pride - how I think others view me
- Pocketbook - the basic desire for money, property, possessions, etc.
- Personal relationship - our relationships with other people
- Ambition - our goals, plans, and designs for the future
- Emotional security - general sense of well-being
- Sex relations - basic drive for sexual intimacy.

(Remember, not all these seven parts of self will apply to every resentment.)

This is a great process with which to see patterns of behavior, as well as the corresponding emotions. For example, one of the first resentments I had on my list was my mom (column 1). One of the things she did that I resented was hold me back in the third grade (column 2). When this happened, it was extremely humiliating (column 3). We had moved to a new school district and I had only completed half of a semester of the third grade (I guess I wasn't killing it academically, ha-ha). I had to repeat the third grade.

Which of the seven parts of self did this affect? Let us go down the list:

Pride – Definitely. I thought everyone now believed I was an idiot.

Pocketbook - Does not apply, it was in the third grade.

Personal relationship – Absolutely! With my mother. I was very angry.

Ambitions - Definitely applies; it was the first time I got the "fuck-its," e.g., "They think I'm stupid, fuck it, I'm not going to even try."

Emotional security - This surely applies. I didn't think much of myself.

Sexual relationship - Does not apply, I was in the third grade.

Now, in the fourth column, we look at what our part was in the resentment. Here we put out of our mind the harms others did to us. Let us look at how you played a part in this resentment. The guidelines are, at any point, were you:

Dishonest?

Selfish?

Self-seeking?

Frightened?

Inconsiderate?

For instance, in the resentment with my mother, my part was that I was frightened. I was scared of how others would see me and how I would go through the rest of my life. As time went on, working a program and looking back, I had the insight to revisit this resentment and find my part a little more deeply. I reversed the roles and put myself in my mother's position. This was not solely her decision, she was going on the recommendation of the school board. She was taking care of six children and doing her best to make good choices for them. So not only did fear play a part, but my not considering what my mother was trying to do was my being selfish as well.

One question people often ask is, "What's the difference between selfish and self-seeking?" Selfish is: "I have something and I'm not willing to part with it. I'm being selfish." Self-seeking is: "You have something I want for myself, and I will do whatever it takes to get it from you."

In my years of sobriety, I've done several inventories of my own and have helped hundreds of other addicts complete theirs. One time, I was working with an individual who was a functional illiterate. This person could not read or write so when it was time for him to write an inventory, I wasn't exactly sure how to proceed. Then the thought came to me: I will sit with this guy and he can tell me his resentments, fears, etc. and I will write it all down. I didn't want him to feel less than or any shame for his disability. This was a process of us meeting over a period of five days and many hours of writing. The point I am making is, there is nothing preventing you from making this Step. If you are dedicated to going through the process, even a disability will not hinder you.

Remember, the only person to truly benefit from this exercise is you. Do not cheat yourself out of an incredible experience because it seems difficult. You cannot really understand the benefit of Step Four until you go through the entire task. It's just one of those things you must *do* to really *get*. To really understand it, you *must* do it. It is a key part of your new practice.

Once you've completed the resentment portion of your inventory you can move on to the fears. In the fear part, we have a good look at our fears and how they are blocking us from growing emotionally and spiritually. (And they are.)

There are also four columns to this. In the first column, we write down just what is the fear. An example of this would be: I have a fear of dying, or staying sober, or drinking again, or intimacy, or public speaking, or of a long-term relationship. Whatever they are, you list your fears in column one. Do nothing in column two until you've completed column one.

In column two, write down: why do I have this fear? Such as: I am afraid of dying because I do not know what comes next. I am afraid of staying sober because I've never done it before and I do not think I'll ever have fun again.

In the third column, you will write down what part of yourself has been affected by this fear.

For example, I have a fear of public speaking, first because I was told I wasn't very smart and, second, because I couldn't read very well. That affected (column three) the following: my self-esteem, pride, emotional security, ambitions and personal relationships.

In the fourth column, write down any action you can take to overcome this fear. That action will be specific to each individual fear. Remember we're looking at the contrary action to your natural inclination to say, "I can't because… _____." Let me say it again: *You cannot think your way into the right action, you need to act your way into the right thinking.* So, think: "I must set a course of action to walk through this fear." The more you do this, the more facing fear becomes a working part of your life.

Early on in my sobriety, I could talk myself out of almost anything. It was all fear-based. "I'm not going to apply for that job. I'm an ex-convict. I'm not smart enough. They will never hire me. There are other people way more qualified than I am." I remember how afraid I was when I was applying for the job at the County

Jail. I was sure that because of my past and my education level, they would not hire me. But I ran it by a few friends and they told me to apply anyway. They encouraged me. So, I went through the motions, told the truth and was completely honest. This turned out in my favor—I got the job! But if I hadn't suited up and shown up, I never would have had this opportunity. Wayne Gretzky, one of the all-time hockey greats, said it perfectly, "You miss 100 percent of the shots you do not take."

An example of fear on your inventory could be: I have a fear of staying sober. So, in column four, I would write:

These are the things I'm going to do daily to stay sober to outgrow my fear:

1. Meditate

2. Read inspirational books

3. Go to a support group

4. Live by a set of principles that are positive

5. Help other people who are less fortunate than I am

To sum it up, in this section of Step Four, we must get it all down on paper; recognize the fear, see how it affected us, and then take the appropriate actions/ contrary actions to outgrow these fears.

In the last section of this inventory, we review our sexual conduct or, if you'd like, how we've acted overall in previous relationships of any kind.

This is basically broken down into five columns.

1) Who did I hurt?

2) What did I do to them?

3) Did I unjustifiably arouse jealousy, suspicion, bitterness?

4) Where was I at fault? Was I selfish, dishonest, inconsiderate?

5) We write down what we could have done instead.

It seems like when I was practicing my disease—drinking and using—any relationship I was in was pretty much dysfunctional. So, when I started my inventory, in the first column for whom I hurt, it was everyone that I'd ever been in a relationship with.

It was as simple as this:

First column: (Who?) The person's name, i.e., "Sue."

Second column: (What did I do?) "I told her I loved her to get sex."

Third column: (Negative emotional impact) "I aroused bitterness, jealousy, and suspicion." (All of these all came up as time went on.)

Fourth column: (Where was my fault?) "I was selfish—I wasn't thinking of her needs. I was dishonest—I lied about being in love. I was inconsiderate—I never thought of how this would affect her, only as a means to my ends."

Fifth column: (What could I have done instead?) I really looked at every person on this list and placed their needs first, to avoid letting my actions cause them any further harm at all.

When I do this, it's not about me anymore. It's about how I can become a better person.

This process goes back to what we talked about earlier in Step Three. Once we become sober and start living the program, we naturally evolve into a higher vibration wherein we cannot continue to hurt people or be dishonest.

Doing this will help us to mold our ideals and to live up to them. We can put ourselves to the test with each new relationship. We can focus on the right ideal and have the program and people who have walked before us give us their guidance in any questionable situation. We are looking to shape a sound ideal for our future relationships, including sex relations.

Step 5

"Admitted to God, to ourselves, and to another human being the exact nature of our wrongs."

Now that we've completed Step Four, the inventory of our resentments, fears, and sexual/romantic relationships—in fact, *all* our interpersonal relationships—we are now ready to sit down with someone we trust, most likely our sponsor, to read and talk about this inventory.

I know, you're asking, "Dave, how do we get around the 'admitting to God' part?" After all, God is one of the first words in this Step! Since we have the other two down, admitting to ourselves and another human being, let us address the God part.

As far as admitting to God goes, this was my experience when I first took this Step: It was about really getting honest with myself. To do that, I trusted the process of taking the Steps. Before I sat down with my sponsor, I sat in silence in my prison bunk reflecting on everything I had written, knowing I was trusting the process, letting go, taking directions from other people such as my sponsor. I never really said, "Okay, God, this is me." This is very subjective. If you have something you've connected with, *that* is what you can meditate on. For me, it was just trusting *a power greater than myself,* which was the program and the 12 Steps.

Exclude the word God if you need to. I don't mean that in a disrespectful way; I mean to set it aside and replace it with something that works for you, like "the universe" or the "program." It's just a word, do not get hung up on it. If it doesn't work, do not throw out the entire Steps—make them work for you.

With Step Five, I can only go on my own experience. When I did my first inventory and sat down with my sponsor to read it to him, I was fully engaged in the process. What I mean is, I was plugged into a power greater than myself—synergy—feeling the love and compassion, and especially trust. I truly believed in and trusted in this process. I knew if I did the Steps, it would change my life. By committing myself to doing this, I had the clear sense that I would not go back to using drugs and alcohol. So, it appeared that I was admitting or committing to a power greater than myself. I still believe it was the power of the program—the love and compassion in the people who participated in my growth process with me. I was going through the process myself but I knew I wasn't alone. I felt the power of the camaraderie of the program.

So, I sat down with my sponsor and we started from the first resentment. The process probably took over two hours from start to finish. He was very patient and never judged me. One of the biggest reasons for doing this with another person is to get an objective view, or what I like to call a "helicopter" view. Someone that is not emotionally attached to any of the content in your inventory is very helpful. This was a very emotional Step for me. I'd never shared a lot of the content of it with any other human being.

It's a very liberating process. My sponsor made some good points to help me process through some of my resentments, fears and patterns, especially in my past relationships. There were a lot of tears and a lot of laughter. Afterwards, I was amazed and a little exhausted from the whole thing. I knew I had completed something. I could begin to trust another human being and I had the beginnings of some confidence in myself. I was starting to change. I was a part of something larger than myself, a power greater than myself. Now, I was really a part of the program. When I think of personal milestones in my life, doing Step Five is at the top of the list. It gave me a feeling of starting to come together as a fully functional adult and to feel whole.

I have written several inventories since that first one long ago. I have also heard probably over one hundred inventories in the thirty years I've been sober. Patterns start to emerge, similarities one cannot help but notice in all of them. In recovery, we're all basically the same—we have the same problems, the same fears, and the same patterns of relationships. We're human beings, and we're not perfect. We remain imperfect even doing the Steps because that is the nature of being human. Instead of striving to become perfect, the goal of our work is love and service to others. That begins with love and care of ourselves. This isn't selfish or narcissistic; it is the start of the endgame: providing more love and joy to others.

A lot of times we'll sense or even hear our inner voice tell us that "more will be revealed." What does that mean? To me, the more I practice this way of living, this new set of principles, the more is revealed to me. I wanted to become this vision of an ideal person I had created in my mind. Again, not a perfect person, but a good and helpful person with compassion and depth. "More will be revealed" also can mean that as you continue your path, you will come to understand life's complexities and the nature of reality in a deeper and more meaningful way.

There had been a significant event in my life, an emotional experience that I had never shared with another human being. I didn't put it into my first inventory because I didn't remember it at the time. Months later, I remembered it and as soon as I did, I needed to talk to someone about it. I called my sponsor, we got together, and I told him the whole story. We processed it thoroughly and then gave it up to the universe. Here I will just say about it that "more will be revealed." (We're peeling layers of an onion here.)

So, Step Five is all about letting go and trusting the process and another human being. If we can "step" back from self-will, and put our trust into the program and another human being, we are changing for the better.

Step 6

*"Were entirely ready to have God remove all these defects
of character."*

The word "God" comes up again in this Step. And, again, we are
speaking of the power that is greater than us that plugs us into this
energetic journey. You've immersed yourself in the program, you
are living by a new set of (higher) principles. That is a power greater
than yourself. Being around people who are involved in right living
motivates us as though through osmosis. This is synergy, the co-
creative power that takes you through this process.

There is no entity or "thing" that will remove your defects of
character. What will happen is that the longer you are on this
path, the longer you work a program, these defects will naturally
become apparent to you and the arising awareness in you makes
them intolerable. It resets your personal standards. It raises them
naturally.

Carl Jung says, in the Big Book chapter "There Is a Solution,"
that a spiritual experience is the change of ideas, emotions, and
attitudes that will be replaced by a whole new set of ideals. He
writes:

*"Alcoholics have what are called vital spiritual experiences. To me
these experiences are phenomena. They appear to be in the nature of
huge emotional displacements and rearrangements. Ideas, emotions,
and attitudes which were once the guiding forces of the lives of these men
are suddenly cast to one side, and a completely new set of conceptions
and motives begin to dominate them."* [2]

---

2   *The Big Book of Alcoholics Anonymous*, page 27.

In the book *Twelve Steps and Twelve Traditions*, it says, "This is the Step that separates [the women from the girls or] the men from the boys."[3] This Step is all about willingness and honesty. If you can look at your behavior and have an honest desire to change, you've already come a long way, spiritually. Throughout our inventory, we've looked for—and found—patterns of behavior, negative things that are not working for us. In the resentment section, we saw how fear, selfishness, self-centeredness, inconsiderate behavior, and anger were dragging us down. Now, with Step Six, we're striving for a new set of principles that inform a more positive way of living our lives, not taking us back to drinking or using.

So, what does that mean, "separates the men from the boys or the women from the girls?" Basically, this means that when we can mature emotionally or grow up and really look at our own patterns of behavior, we can then take full responsibility for our own actions. The biggest thing we talk about in this program is "change." As I've said before, you hear it said in meetings, "There's only one thing that you have to change and that is everything." That always makes me laugh; the sweeping scope of it is so overwhelming. You say to yourself, "Well, that's just great. I have to change my entire life? Sure, no problem!"

Obviously, this too is a process, a practice we strive for; it doesn't happen overnight. We really must have the willingness and honesty to look at ourselves and say, "Yes, I need to change." That compels you to wake up to your life and want something better for yourself and all the people around you. This disease affects everyone you encounter—your parents, your family, your employer, your friends. Now they tell us alcohol was a *symptom*. We must get down to the cause and condition of what brought us to our knees. If we're not willing to change or even look at our behaviors, we could end up back to drinking and using.

---

3   *The 12 Steps & Twelve Traditions*, page 63.

What, exactly, is a "defect of character?" Think about how you have acted in the past and what qualities and actions no longer serve you. One of the big ones for me was trust. I had a hard time trusting anyone, in the program or outside the program. In the life that I came from, drinking and using, everyone was out for themselves. I didn't trust anyone.

One thing that helped me to work towards a new life and trust other people was when someone said to me, "It is no longer your story. That story of suffering and lack and victimhood. You have a new and wonderful beginning." That little statement had a big impact on me.

Little by little, I stopped suspecting that people were trying to get one over on me. I looked at them with less distrust and more interest and realized that of course they weren't all out to get me.

If you look in the Big Book on page 76, where Steps Six and Seven are outlined, it does not give you much explanation or direction on this Step. One of the reasons for this, I believe, is that perhaps Bill Wilson didn't fully understand it either.

I say this because fourteen years after the Big Book was first published, Bill Wilson wrote *Twelve Steps and Twelve Traditions*. In this text, he gives a better explanation of Step Six, as well as direction on how to take this Step. Essentially, it is, as we said, about getting honest and looking closely at the behaviors that don't work in your life. And, also that at this point, you must be *willing* to change them, give them up, and commit to be ready for the next level of the process.

Here, too, the question, "How do we get around the God aspect of the Steps?" comes up. Remember, we're working with energy; the power greater than ourselves is the process of *working the steps*. We are striving to live a more loving, compassionate, serene life. We're connecting with the power greater than ourselves—synergy—by going through the process, looking into ourselves, wanting genuine, honest change. This is no magic trick. This is about uncovering, discovering, discarding. It's about doing the work.

Let us take the example of *uncover, discover, discard*. This is in reference to any character defect or problem in our life.

First and foremost, we must *uncover* the problem. Say the behavior is lying or being dishonest. We uncover this problem, admit that we have it and admit that it's causing a problem in our life. When we uncover it, our work is to get honest.

Discover means bringing the problem into the light of day. We were as sick as our secrets. We bring it into the light of day by discussing it with another person. Honesty about our dishonesty loosens its grip on us.

Discard is the process of recognizing that whenever this problem or character defect crops up again, we do not have to do it. We can *choose* to be honest instead. Once we recognize this behavior, then we change it.

For this Step, my sponsor sat down with me, and frankly, he didn't explain it very well. I'd been locked up close to three years at that point. He took out his business card and wrote down the Seven Deadly Sins, all of which I'd been intimately acquainted with in my life, sometimes all at the same time: anger, greed, pride, lust, gluttony, sloth, envy.

Sins are basically bad behavior or decisions, so to sin literally means to miss the mark. Drop the religious connotation and insert my definition here, so it will work for you. *To sin is to miss the mark.*

My sponsor said, "When these crop up in your life, take a look at them, see how you can change these defects. This is something we strive for, perfect ideals. These are goals we work towards. They are the measuring sticks by which we estimate our progress."

I looked at the Seven Deadly Sins he had written down on his business card (I do not think I'd ever really looked at these before) and the one that jumped out at me was lust. I'd been locked up for a long time and a lot of what I thought about was lustful. When he said removing lust as one of the Seven Deadly Sins, I thought he meant not having sex with anybody. I thought, well I'm just not ready to give that up yet. Please! But he didn't mean giving it up at all. He meant that if my lustful behavior was controlling my life, if it distracts me or takes me off the spiritual path of living by a new set of principles, then it's a problem.

I tried to visualize how this would work. Finally, I came up with this model: If you're driving along and see someone you think is very good looking, you say to yourself, "Wow! That person is really hot or beautiful!" And you continue down the street. That is a moderate example of being lustful. An extreme example would be, "Wow, do you see that person? She's very hot!" You stop the car and tell her, "You're a very beautiful person, would you like to come with me?" And you do not take "no" for an answer. This could become problematic. I actually know of someone who was, in fact, driving when a particularly lust-inducing person crossed the street. Next thing he knew, he smacked into the car in front of him.

If your behavior overall affects your life and others in a negative way, you must admit it, examine it and change that behavior—whatever the shortcoming or character defect is. Step Six all comes down to being *entirely ready*. That was what I needed. Again, this is about recognizing a behavior that is not working for us, just like drugs and alcohol were not working for us. *Until we realize what's causing us significant pain and problems, we aren't really willing to change.* Not that we want to wait for a behavior to cause pain and problems, but chances are that it already exists, you just haven't recognized and admitted it yet, especially if it's causing others pain. This must be some kind of bug in the human system: until a behavior is causing a serious problem, we will not change it. Things can continue to work in lopsided, dysfunctional ways for a while without really working. Then we get it and can no longer stand to be a person who causes harm to others.

The question to ask yourself is, "Am I entirely ready to look at myself honestly?" Remember, anything that is learned can be unlearned. And most of the patterns of behavior in our life are learned behaviors. A lot of people say, "That is just the way I am," which is mostly bullshit. That's a convenient way to both continue a behavior that is not very healthy and dismiss its impact on yourself and others. I taught a class where a student actually said to me, "Well that is how my great grandma did it, that is how my grandma did it, that is how my mother did it, so that is how I'll do it." My response to this young woman was, "Did you ever think it was the wrong way to do this, if it keeps causing problems?"

Sometimes we must step outside of ourselves, with others' direction, to recognize these unhealthy behaviors. To her point, no, these "sins" or behaviors are not built into your essential genetic makeup. In fact, there are only five things nearly all mammals do which *are* built into our DNA and none of them are learned behaviors. They are: to seek and obtain food, to seek and obtain shelter, to seek and obtain water, to protect the young, and to procreate. We do not have to think about these too much. If we're hungry, we eat; if we're hot or if we're cold, we seek shelter.

Going back to behavioral patterns, looking at the Seven Deadly Sins, all of us have sins or behaviors at some level. Most of the time we keep them in the balance, but other times we fall back into the form and energy of our lower self and the defects and shortcomings start blaring again.

When there's no control or balance to the Seven Deadly Sins, the result affects both your behavior in life and the well-being of others. It's the difference between anger and abuse. Everyone gets angry, but if you get so angry that you become violent and cause harm to others, you become abusive. You are way out of balance. This is another great example of how we can change our behavior because anything learned can be unlearned. In anger management classes, they teach you that life is 10 percent what happens and 90 percent how you react to what happens. If something is getting you so frustrated that you cannot control your temper and blow up at someone, you really must look at *why* you're getting so angry. Does whatever is happening in the moment that makes you so angry really match the situation? Is your response proportional to the trigger? Is it so big of a deal that you must cause problems for yourself and other people? Personally, I like to use the "Twenty-four-hour rule." I might get an upsetting email or phone call, something from a client or my boss. The knee-jerk reaction is usually not very productive. Yet, if I say to myself, let me wait 24 hours to respond to this after I've calmed down a bit, I can have a more objective view of what's happening. Then my reaction or response is not only much calmer, it's way more productive. When what was such a big deal yesterday becomes a much smaller problem today, usually I can deal with it. Trust me, this processing mechanism is not built into my DNA, it is a learned behavior, a conscious change from behavior I could no longer tolerate when I realized its impact on others. What we do *matters*, whether it's benevolent or destructive.

Another example of being out of balance is sparked by the expression, "Money is the root of all evil." It's actually *the love of money* that can be the root of dysfunction. If you're so obsessed with making money, all you do is work (or day trade). Think about how this causes issues in your family life, social life, and spirituality, as well as your own growth. Another example: if you're so concerned about other people—what they have, and how happy they are— you cannot focus on your own behavior and your own progress. A lot of times we judge our insides against other people's outsides. Sometimes I'll see someone who has all the material status and think that I am less-than because I'm not at their level of wealth or achievement. But I have no idea what's *actually* going on in their life—they could be suffering with all kinds of family, emotional, spiritual, or physical pain. Twelve Steppers know this is so; we hear it all the time in meetings.

So, we seek balance. We all want to feel good, be loved, and be able to give love. We started using drugs and alcohol to feel good. Then it became a problem because we have a chemical imbalance (our body's allergy). Step Six is all about recognizing patterns of behavior—the behaviors that are working in your life, and the ones that aren't. This is a new beginning; this is a new story you are creating.

What happens with a lot of us is that we default to the old story because it's comfortable, even though it's dysfunctional. Now, when a negative behavior crops up, we want to think, "How will this benefit me? How can this benefit other human beings?" It's not like you'll never be angry again or lustful, or you will not ever worry. It's about recognizing and being able to change, being entirely ready to have these defects of character removed from your life.

I share this story a lot because it helps me recognize when I'm behaving incorrectly. A friend of mine was helping me rebuild a clutch in my truck. (Disclaimer: I'm not a mechanic, but I'm a great helper.) He showed me something called the "slave cylinder." He said that, when driving, most people will rest their foot on the clutch which engages the slave cylinder and eventually wears out the clutch, thus damaging the vehicle. When you're keeping your foot on the clutch, knowing that you're causing a negative effect to the car, stop. *Just take your foot off.*

This tutorial helped me to see I'm not perfect; I will make mistakes, I will occasionally forget and absently rest my foot on the clutch. We all do. So, it becomes very important to recognize when you're engaging in one of your character fallibilities and then change your behavior. Do not be a slave to it. Be entirely ready to remove all defects of character. This is about progress, not perfection. The more you practice this way of living, the easier it will get! Practice does not make perfect, practice *is* perfect.

Step 7

"Humbly asked Him to remove our shortcomings."

Or, as I would offer:

"Humbly worked (practiced) to remove our shortcomings," drawing on the synergy of the group and the power of going through the Steps process together."

Since this Step concerns itself primarily with humility, first let us investigate what it means to be humble. What is humility and how does it relate to our shortcomings? This is the next phase of the process of changing the way we behave. Which, in turn, will change the way we think.

Dictionary.com defines humility as: "A modest opinion or estimate of one's own importance, rank, etc." Some other words to describe humility are: lack of vanity and modesty. It is the opposite of arrogance and conceit, with which we may have lived our lives up to now. We can change and when we do, it feels great.

We can begin to understand humility by first realizing that our shortcomings and character defects are one and the same. We are flawed human beings. In fact, that is redundant; humans are flawed by definition. It takes something to have enough humility to stare a character defect or shortcoming in the face. The willingness to take an honest look at how you can change it is huge in the process of treating your addiction or alcoholism.

Getting real about our shortcomings means not looking the other way when this behavior or character defect crops up. This is being able to look your issue straight in the eye and say, "I am humbly ready to change. I'm ready to remove all my defects and shortcomings." It sounds so corny to say but we're growing up. We are changing in a profound sense—we're taking direction from other people. This takes a lot of emotional maturity. It is the opposite of saying, "I drink because I'm an alcoholic. There's no need to change it." Popeye comes to mind: "I am what I am." (And this is why Popeye never evolved.) When you commit yourself to changing for the better, this is real growth.

Being humble is about taking responsibility for one's own behavior. It's not always easy, but it sure is worth it. Let me pass along the Asshole Rule: "If you meet one asshole per day, it's probably them. If you meet more than one, it's probably you."

Step Seven is about not blaming anyone for your behavior or your situation. This is about taking an honest self-appraisal and then being able to say: these are my faults, I recognize them and I'm willing to work on changing them.

Remember, this is a process. Nothing happens overnight. The more we practice self-honesty and recognize and change our shortcomings, the more humility becomes a natural, working part of our lives.

For instance, in the process of my own recovery, things have been revealed to me over the years. I believe that in early recovery, the reason I didn't notice certain behaviors was because I wasn't ready or wasn't able to change them at that time. You can't change what you don't admit or are even aware of. The more I learn, the more I want to continue learning and striving for perfection, even knowing that there is no endgame or goal line, that it's just a process. And, we can take this process as far as we want. We can go as deep into our psyche as we want. Or, not. If our behavior continues to harm other people, including ourselves, we *need* to take a humble approach to change this behavior. I believe everything we do matters; the tone of voice we take with people, the food we eat, where we shop, how we conduct ourselves in meetings and in daily life, *it all matters*. So, in one sense, Step 7 is about becoming completely conscious of what's happening in our lives and being mindful of our shortcomings when they crop up.

As your consciousness grows, every behavior matters a little more. That is what program old-timers mean when they say, "*The road gets narrower.*" When you've been working this process and you have a thought or do an action that is of a lower vibration, you will notice it. It will not be the same as before when you had such a wide avenue in which to be more accepting of your character defects.

By working a program, by humbly wanting to change, we become more grateful for the process and the synergy we have now plugged into. I'll say it again, "*You cannot think your way into the right action, you need to act your way into the right thinking.*" A program of action, not thinking, means changing behaviors, becoming humble, getting real, growing up, spiritually and emotionally, not blaming other people for our problems. You have to look the world, no, the *universe*, in the eye, and *want* an honest change. This is like the surrender we took in Step One, but instead of simply admitting that our lives have become unmanageable, we surrender the behaviors that make it so. They don't work for us anymore. Humility is finally accepting the parts of ourselves that are questionable and wanting and allowing them to change.

In the book *Drop the Rock* by Bill P. and Todd, they talk about active surrender. Active surrender is as it sounds; it's not a passive surrender of just giving up the behavior, it's about taking the appropriate *action* to *change* the behavior, and being able to look at this humbly and honestly. The authors list certain values and actions that can help us make the changes in our defects or shortcomings. Remember, we're taking direction, we're working with people for a positive change which creates the synergy to propel us forward.

Some of the actions they list are:

- Spiritual values
- Service
- Perspective beyond our addiction to alcohol, drugs, food, sex and so on, the addictive nature of our lives
- Asking for help and being willing to receive it through humility
- Overcoming fear
- Understanding and trusting the process
- Dealing with stress
- Responsibility/ Action
- Solution-focused thinking

By taking the appropriate action to look humbly at ourselves, we change. Working with other people such as your sponsor, if you're completely honest with him or her, can help you identify certain behaviors that are no longer beneficial to you (if they ever were). Action, action, and more action!

As they say in Buddhist teachings: "What do we do when we reach enlightenment? Chop wood, carry water. What do we do when we haven't yet reached enlightenment? Chop wood, carry water." In other words, just keep up with the process. An example of chop wood, carry water, for me is that no matter what I'm going through, I still practice the principles of the program, even if I do not want to. I have my daily rituals of reading and meditation. I do the next right thing, even when I do not want to do it. I act spiritual, even when I do not feel spiritual. I go to meetings when I do not want to go. I also go to meetings when I want to go to meetings. This is what I mean when I say, "Chop wood, carry water." Carry on.

I've gone through some amazing things in my recovery and some horrific experiences. I went through an awful divorce and, at times, I would find myself in such depression and distress that I would sit for hours and just cry. I knew that no matter what, I had to stay on the path, even if I didn't feel like it, even if I felt like giving up. I tried to always take the high road and never engage in negativity. I surrounded myself with people in recovery who supported me. These were the ways of being that got me through the tough times. I felt the love and synergy.

Changing behaviors is about taking contrary action—when you see something is not working, change it, do the opposite. Remember (or learn) the St. Francis prayer. This is not about magic. This is about wanting to do the right thing. It may seem weird to include a Saint's prayer in a book about recovery without naming God, but I have always taken these words to help people live their best lives. As I worked the Steps with my sponsor, I saw this less as a prayer

Indonesia, 2006. Living the dream in recovery. My addiction took away two things I loved — surfing and playing music. My recovery gave them back to me.

and more as a means to spur contrary action to my old ways. And, as an *intention*. It became a spiritual experience for me in the sense that it caused a change in my perception and experience. I hope it can do the same for you.

Prayer of St. Francis of Assisi
Make me an instrument of your peace.
Where there is hatred, let me sow love.
Where there is injury, pardon.
Where there is doubt, faith.
Where there is despair, hope.
Where there is darkness, light.
Where there is sadness, joy.
Grant that I may not so much seek to be consoled, as to console
To be understood, as to understand
To be loved, as to love
For it is in giving, that we receive
It is in pardoning, that we are pardoned.
It is in dying that we are born into eternal life.

I once thought of these lines as, "How can I change the outside world?" But when I looked at it in reference to my own behaviors, that is when the real change came about. When I felt hatred, I changed that energy to love. When I felt resentment, I changed that to forgiveness, and so on. This is a very powerful Step. If you're humbly ready to look at some behaviors that need to be changed, you're making major progress. Chop wood, carry water.

Cleaning House, Part 2

Step 8: Change
Step 9: Integrity

CHAPTER 5

Cleaning House, Part 2

———

In this chapter, we continue with the next steps that complete the important Middle Six (Steps 3-9). These Steps intensify our understanding of humility and forgiveness and, most importantly, put them into action to help repair the damage we did on the way down to hitting bottom.

Step 8

"We made a list of all persons we had harmed, and became willing to make amends to them all."

Step Eight is keeping with the theme of action, action and more action. Most people freak out about this Step because they're already thinking of Step Nine. Do not think about Step Nine yet! If you can stay present in this moment and just work on this Step, it will go easily and quickly.

All they're asking of us is to write down a list. We can take a lot of the names from our Fourth Step, especially in the relationship/sex section of the inventory. In the first column of the sex inventory, they ask us, "Who did we harm?" So that makes it easy. We can also look at the resentment section of our Step Four to see if any of those names would fit on our amends list.

We started this process by saying we would go to any lengths for our recovery. Well, that willingness to go forward is a big part of Step Eight.

First, let us define the word *amends*. A lot of people think this is a Step where we are saying that we are sorry for our past behavior. This is partly true, but if we look up the true meaning of the word "amend," another definition is to "change" something.[4]

For example, when we have an amendment to a contract or a legal document, we're changing it in some way. One of the best examples is an amendment to the U.S. Constitution. Amends in Step Eight include both saying you're sorry and making a change to your behavior, a behavior that hopefully you will not repeat. Change is the optimum word here. Change is having a spiritual experience. Where we acted one way before, now we're behaving in a more positive and compassionate way. We have changed our *perception*.

Let us also look at the word *harm*. Someone can do physical harm, psychological (thinking) harm, and emotional (feeling) harm. Harm can be done to another person, as well as to animals, to the planet, and to ourselves. Obviously, people can suffer physical (bodily) harm when they're attacked. They suffer psychological or emotional harm when people gossip about them, spread rumors or lies about them and harangue, humiliate or belittle them. The damage can be incalculable and those who cause it sometimes never realize how deep the impact was until they look closely at who they owe amends.

Write down the list and subject each and every situation, person, place, or thing to the test. Have you created harm? How? Then there are the financial amends. (That was a big one for me. I never thought I would get over that.) Again, we're just writing a list. We're

---

4   www.dictionary.cambridge.org/us/dictionary/english/amend

not making any direct amends yet, we're just getting it all down on paper. So, if you owe $10 or $10 million, it does not matter. Write it all down.

Some of the obvious amends needed will be to our immediate family, employers, friends, and the county, state, and country in which we live.

When I first wrote my list, it was so long and involved that my sponsor suggested I write *three* lists. The first list was people to whom I would absolutely make amends. The second list was people to whom I would possibly make amends, and the third list was people to whom I would never make amends. I believed there were some people in my life during my active addiction and alcoholism who did more harm to *me* than I did to them. I thought, it's just a wash, or we're even, no need to go there. But as my sponsor pointed out to me, this is not *their* program, this is *my* program. No matter what I believed someone did to me, I focused only on the amends *I* needed to make to the person to whom *I* caused harm.

When you write your list, do it in two columns.

In the first column, list to whom or what (an institution or place) you owe amends. In the second column, list what happened and why do you owe amends?

I always like to start with the first column, and just work on that. I take the names off my Fourth Step, and then write additional names as needed. Again, I just do it vertically in the first column. When I finish it, I move onto the second column: What did I do to cause them harm?

When you have completed your list, take the next action step: set a time to meet with your sponsor. Go over each amends with him or her and ask for and receive their direction on how to approach each unique situation. This process has been very helpful for me and also sometimes surprising. For example, my sponsor once told me to hold off doing some of the amends on my list for a while. I explained that I was "willing" to go to any lengths to change! But there were some people on the list that I couldn't reach; they may have even passed away. My sponsor gave me explicit direction on each amends and I carefully followed them.

Making the list is always an exciting process. And no wonder: you declare your intent to admit, apologize and repair mistakes that have weighed you down with shame in the past. You're making a change, and change means an awakening is taking place. You are plugged into a loving, compassionate, and forgiving energy. When you stay close and do the work well, you will not be disappointed; you *will* feel like you're living in a new dimension. You are! We are no longer vibrating in our lower selves, we are now vibrating at a higher frequency as we work with intention towards the Highest version of ourselves.

Once you have completed this list, you will have made great progress.

Let us keep going, shall we?

Step 9

"Made direct amends to such people whenever possible, except when to do so would injure them or others."

Now you can freak out about Step Nine. Just kidding. You are completely prepared for it. Your list is completed, you've met with your sponsor, he or she has given you complete instructions on what to do. This is where the rubber meets the road, so to speak.

It can be a little intimidating—and very humbling—to see all the names written down: the people, places, and things you've harmed. Step Nine holds tremendous power: this is the first time we step outside the program to approach people who are not necessarily in a 12-Step program or working on a spiritual path.

As you know, it's a good idea to have a non-emotional, objective view (helicopter view) of things. It is said that there are three sides to any story: my side, your side, and *what really happened.* Your sponsor can give you feedback based on their own Step Nine experiences. Your sponsor isn't emotionally involved in your amends list so their objectivity is key. When I first sat down with my sponsor and read my amends list to him, he suggested several things I hadn't thought of, going into this. It's good to have an objective, outside opinion, much as a therapist would provide for your mental well-being.

Let me share just a few examples that might be helpful for making your amends.

Nine times out of ten, amends will go better than expected. But there are times when they do not go so well.

When I made an amends to my uncle, for instance, he didn't accept either my apology or my stated intention to change my behavior. I did some awful things to him. I stole some of his possessions and lied about it when I was caught. I was deep into my addiction at the time. Early in my sobriety, I went to see my uncle and aunt to work this amends Step with them directly. My aunt was also on the list and when I made amends to her, she was very loving and forgiving. I took my uncle off to the side privately and attempted to explain. His response was not favorable—to say the least. He said to me, "What you did to our family is something I will never forgive. I would appreciate it if you would stay away from our family. *Do not contact us again.*" He couldn't have made his feelings any clearer. I honored his wishes and never saw him again. He passed away. But I did see my aunt once more, on her deathbed. I was able to be present for her while she passed and finally, years later, felt that I had redeemed myself by doing so.

Again, Step Nine does not rest on whether your amends are accepted, forgiven or even understood. This is about you being willing to clean your side of the street and to know that you've done your best to right a wrong. Step Nine frees you. You are now able to walk anywhere on this planet, free of shame, knowing you have done your part.

Another thing to note; do not involve another party in this process. For instance, if you were unfaithful in your relationship and that is an amends you're making, it is not appropriate or fair to include the person with whom you've cheated, by naming them or otherwise. No matter how much your partner might press you.

But let's back up here for a minute. When a friend of mine first read that paragraph, she peppered me with questions: "Wait, what if your partner says it's not a real amend without full disclosure? What if she or he *needs* that information to feel healed? Does a half-truth make you only half-honest? What if you're protecting the person you cheated with at your partner's expense? What if they perceive an omission as a lie? David! These conversations happen all the time! Plus, the information you're not giving your partner may be found on social media—that can blow your amends wide open!"

She wrapped up with, "I'm just sayin'."

I considered this. I'd had my belief about not involving other names in an amends for being unfaithful for a long time. It was my sponsor's direction. But I could see her point. People to whom you're making this particular amends may ask for the information for the reasons my friend listed, or others, if you are still in an active relationship. Trying to rebuild trust is hard. Many of us, especially millennials, have left social media footprints. I gave this a lot of thought.

What I think is that this advice calls for a case-by-case situation assessment. If you think this information is helpful and not harmful, then get your sponsor's objective views on it. But I do still believe that taking full responsibility for the harm *you* caused means that *you and only you* own it.

As you work the Middle Six Steps, you're making important changes in your life. You've changed your behavior by your willingness and humility *to even do this work*. It's hard. It helps to keep remembering that this is a program of change.

Sometimes change comes slowly. As they say, "Change is a process, not an event." That is the truth. And you have to be ready and willing to let yourself be changed. In my own case, I had never made a list of people whom I'd harmed or injured when I was still using and to whom I wanted to make amends before I did the Middle Six Steps. I had said "Sorry" a lot, but I'd never changed my behavior. I didn't have a program that gave me guidelines or a set of principles by which to live. We do the work and we get a result, it's just that simple. As I've said before, we are now vibrating at a different, higher level. We place ourselves in situations that are positive, not negative. We're willing to help other people, we're connected to the synergy as our Higher Selves. We do not have to duck and dodge anyone or anything. We can look the world in the eye and say: I'm walking on the sunny side of the street. I've done my part now, that is all I can do. We feel liberated.

There are so many ways to make an amends. What they require of us is far beyond a simple, "I'm sorry." (Though they should always include at least one.) Besides actions to repair the damage we caused, we also make amends so our behavior does not create more harm. We are going to look squarely at how we've hurt people emotionally, financially, physically, or psychologically. This is something most people will never brave in their lifetime.

It's usually a good idea to start with our immediate family.

I wrote out my list of amends while I was still incarcerated. My mother and father were big ones on my list. My mother, especially, because she was in the program. My sponsor and I came up with an idea. Precisely the day after I was released, my mother went to an early morning AA meeting at the church. I attended the meeting and asked her to come into the chapel with me afterwards. There, I made my amends.

It was very emotional; we both cried. I told her I was committed to the program and to making a change in my life. She died six years later, seeing her son with seven years of sobriety. I was able to be present when she was dying, to help her pass into the other side. It was one of the greatest and saddest events of my life. The good news is that my behavior changed and I was able to be a responsible, loving son to my mother in the last years of her life.

The amends with my father were a little different. He was not in the program and not naturally inclined to be as emotionally present as my mother. His emotional IQ wasn't anywhere near hers. So, making amends to my dad presented a communications challenge. When I did my amends to him, he kept asking me if I was through using and drinking. I would say things like, "One day at a time" or "As long as I work a program." He wanted to see it as yes or no, black or white. He kept pressing me, saying, "I'm not so much concerned with that. *Are you through with using and drinking?*" I finally realized I had to communicate in *his* language. When I said, "Yes, Dad, I'm done," he finally smiled and gave me a hug.

It went well with all my siblings, too. I think everyone was a little skeptical about my ability to stay sober and it was up to me to prove that I could by living by a set of principles. I had the ability to change. If the prospect of sobriety for the rest of your life seems overwhelming, it's wise to remember that sustainability happens one day at a time. You may have to educate people like my dad who want a definitive declaration or a promise or some "proof" that they can count on you to follow through. Help them see the process as we do: a way of living every day with an intent to remain sober and a mindfulness of the impact we have on others. There are no guarantees. We make our own realities anew each day.

If you think you have done some bad things to people who you could never face again, let me share a story with you.

The first time I ever went to jail I was fourteen-years-old. There was a drug on the street called "reds." They were Seconal barbiturates. You could buy them at the high school or on the streets. They came in packs of ten capsules. They were so potent that you could take one or two and feel like you'd drank a whole bottle of wine. Really dangerous.

My friends and I would take reds *and* drink wine. The wine was either Spanada or Red Mountain. Both were so horrible and would get you so fucked up, that taking reds on top of it was just incredibly crazy. (Now I see that, whereas I once thought this made us somewhat "typical teenagers.")

One day, we all were hanging out at the dead-end street near my friend Kevin's house, where we all used to hang out, drinking, smoking pot, taking reds, the usual. Back then, we wore flannel t-shirts, ripped up blue jeans, and steel toe motorcycle boots—all of us were in uniform. Kind of like a James Dean thing.

I was hanging out with my friend Rob, who is now doing life in prison for bank robbery. We were hungry so we decided we would break into Kevin's house to get something to eat. We knew nobody was home. Logical plan, right?

Kevin's house was a typical Southern California tract home, set close to the street. We approached the house and snuck around to the back. Rob got a rock and threw it through the back-door window, then stuck his hand through the jagged glass opening to jimmy the lock. The moment the rock landed with a crash inside, Rob and I looked at each other with fear and excitement in our eyes. For me, this was the moment of no return.

The reds and wine we'd consumed both started coming on strong when we were inside the house. For some reason, I started kicking holes in the wall with my steel-toe boots and broke the stairway banister. I must have been in a semi-blackout by then, to have started vandalizing the house.

Then, I found a twenty-two-caliber rifle in the closet and started shooting bullets into the walls. Rob found the father's Playboy magazines. He then proceeded to pass out on the couch with his ripped up blue jeans around his ankles.

This was not some random house, this was Kevin, our good buddy's house. We knew the family was gone for the day; to make things worse, we found out later that they'd been at their grandmother's funeral. Amidst all the chaos of this mess we were making, I heard a car in the driveway. They were home early!

I woke Rob up and clumsily we tried to hide in the closet. He was trying to hold his breath and vomited a small explosion, some out of his nose, of red colored barf all over our white T-shirts. We heard all of them, mom, dad, their daughter, the aunt, the uncle, gasping with shock, with Kevin silently trailing behind them as they came into the house.

"What's that noise?!" We heard one of the family members approaching.

I was trying to be quiet in the closet but I was so messed up, I fell over, taking Rob down with me, knocking the door to our pathetic hiding place wide open.

Kevin's father looked down at us accusingly. His face turned red with rage. He then got out a twelve-gauge shotgun, pointed it at us, and tried to pull us to our feet by our hair. Neither Rob nor I could stand up.

Next, as far as I could recall, he dragged us downstairs into the living room; meanwhile, the family was screaming and crying in disbelief at what we had done. They were so disturbed and upset to find their home in such a condition—I will never forget their anguish. It took everything they had to not wring our necks.

Kevin's sister yelled, "Dad! Call the police!" And he did.

I could not attempt to communicate with the family because I was so out of my mind, I couldn't speak. By then, I couldn't even see—my vision had blurred out entirely.

It turned into a neighborhood scene. All the neighbors were out on their front lawns. The sheriff's patrol cars came flashing their lights and sirens. Rob and I were a shameful spectacle. The police roughly pulled us out onto the front lawn and handcuffed us with their boots on our backs while we lay face down in the dirt.

I can still hear the family wailing. Imagine coming home from burying your grandmother and finding two completely intoxicated teenage boys who had just destroyed your home.

By the time we got to jail, I was in a full black-out. The police called our parents. They moved us to juvenile hall. The next day, they released us to our parents. I don't think the magnitude of what we'd done had hit us yet. But then came the court proceedings. I was charged with two felony counts: felony breaking and entering, as well as a felony under the influence of dangerous drugs. If it wasn't for my father getting me an attorney, I would have ended up in Y.A. (youth authority, adolescent prison). Instead, I was sentenced to three months in a "bad boy" camp in Spokane, Washington.

I bring this up not to tell you how my criminal career started, but how making amends begins with the pain of memories like this one. And I was only fourteen.

I got sober at age thirty-three. I was in the process of working the 12 Steps. When I got to Step Eight, I carefully read the instructions. It said, "Write a list of all persons you have harmed and become willing to make amends to them all."

Diligently, I went through my life and made an exhaustive effort to write down each and every person I had ever wronged. I made a sincere effort to get in touch with all of the people on my list to make these amends. And you guessed it, Kevin's entire family was on my amends list.

It was 1989, twenty years after I wrecked their home, and I had no idea how to get in touch with these people. Remember, this is pre-internet, pre-Facebook, pre-social media. I was willing to make amends to them, but I had no idea how to contact them. It weighed on my mind for years until a friend of mine, Lance, who was part of that same group of friends with Kevin when we were teenagers, was visiting California. It must have been 2002 or 2003 by then. Lance, himself, had gotten sober in the 90s and was then living in Costa Rica. We reconnected and rekindled our friendship, now as brothers in recovery.

One night, out of the blue, he called me up and said, "We have to do a 12-Step call on an old friend of ours who is living in Carlsbad."

A 12-Step call is when a person is intoxicated or struggling with their sobriety, possibly in danger, and someone, usually in their immediate family, calls a program member on their behalf. There is an unwritten rule that you never go on a 12-Step call by yourself; it's a vulnerable situation with a person who is likely still under the influence.

The "old friend" of mine and Lance's who was in trouble turned out to be Kevin. Lance was nervous to confront him because Kevin was still drinking and using. He asked me if I would go with him.

Now, this wasn't down the street from my house, mind you, I was living about three and a half hours north of Carlsbad. I nonetheless immediately agreed and drove down to Southern California to meet him. (This is what you do for your fellow alcoholics/addicts, even if it's an inconvenience in your life. And you always end up being glad you could help. Always.)

When we arrived at Kevin's house, he was in quite a state. He was in his underwear screaming and yelling obscenities on the front lawn of his house in an upper middle-class neighborhood. His wife was in tears and afraid (to say the least) and asked us if we could please take him away from the house.

This was the start of a very bizarre weekend.

Toward evening, we drove around town trying to find a room. Everything was booked. Finally, we found one motel room that had a single queen bed for all of us. We checked in and Lance and I dragged Kevin into the room. He was so intoxicated that he fell down on the bed and passed out. Lance and I were so exhausted that we lay down next to him and actually managed to get a little sleep.

It can be really comfortable snuggling with your buddies. Or not. Kevin snored so loud all night. The next morning, he had a bad hangover, but he was sober.

We got some food in him and took him straight to a 12-Step meeting. But during the meeting, Lance and I looked up and Kevin was gone. He had simply left the meeting. It took us hours to find him; he had been wandering the streets. We'd driven up and down every boulevard in town. He was nowhere to be seen. Finally, out of the corner of my eye I saw someone talking to a homeless guy. Of course, it was Kevin. By then, he had acquired some more alcohol and was completely inebriated again. We managed to get him in the car, brought him back to the motel, cleaned him up, and put him to bed.

The following day, he woke up and asked if we could take him to his mother's house. Here was my chance at last. The synergy was in effect for me to finally make amends to the matriarch of the family (the father had passed away by this time). I walked into the same house I'd trashed thirty years before and there was an elderly woman with white hair sitting in a chair I remembered, staring up at me.

I felt so uncomfortable and anxious, I had no idea what was going to happen next. My words were choked-up already. I was a much different person than the boy who'd been there years earlier. I was sober, in recovery, working to become a responsible member of society.

I looked down at Kevin's mother, a lump in my throat, tears in my eyes, and I said to her, "Hello, Mrs. Smith, my name is David Vartabedian. I do not know if you remember me."

She looked me straight in the eye and said, "Oh yes, I remember you. How could I forget?"

I felt like time was standing still and there was no one else in the room but her and me.

I said to her, "I've turned my life around. I no longer use drugs and alcohol. I'm doing much better. What I did to your family when I was a little, awful teenager, there's no excuse for. I have thought of what I've done to you and your family every day since I've gotten sober.

"I've wanted to make amends to you for years but didn't know how to get in touch with you. It has been weighing heavily on my heart. If there was any way I could take back what I did to you and your family, I would. I am terribly sorry and I would truly understand if you threw me out of your house right now."

By this time, tears were flowing freely down my face. I felt deep love and compassion for this elderly woman.

At that moment, she looked up at me, and said, "I forgive you."

I believe we were both set free at that moment. The power I felt is what I talk about as synergy. Love was present and the healing had begun with this forgiveness. She was so happy that I was there to help her son. I had an immediate *knowing* there was a shift happening in my life.

Kevin and I stayed in contact for the next several years. He did manage to stay sober and was working a program. He seemed happy; he moved to Montana and his life was getting better. Sadly, I found out a few years ago that Kevin had passed away from a sudden heart attack.

The gift of the program was that he and I had made our own amends to each other, and we were complete. There was no ill will, nothing left unsaid or any lingering resentments on either of our parts. Our friendship had survived a terrible betrayal and treacherous addiction. In the end, we were able to reconcile because of the program. Rest in peace, my dear friend.

This is what I mean when I say that there is a *power* in working these Steps. The power does not necessarily have to have a name like "God" or any other label to be effective. It's about working through it, humbling yourself, and taking the right and appropriate actions. You can't help but feel and see the change within yourself.

Living by a new set of principles based on love and service gives you a feeling, a joy, beyond words. You are now connecting to a higher vibration. It's what we call recovery.

......

I benefitted in no small part by the direction my sponsor would give me on making an amends. He counseled me to do mine in a general way, rather than refer to specific events that happened. It's best to review what happened in a general way, he explained, so we don't get into a back-and-forth about what did or did not happen and switch the focus from the amends to what happened in the past. It's also important not to pull other people into the drama.

As long as we bring willingness and intention to the amends, I've found, there will likely be success. I would say something like this to address my transgressions generally: "When I was drinking and using, my behavior was awful. I did things that were completely unacceptable. I am now working a program that has given me tools to make a change in my life and not go back to drinking and using. I want you to know I am truly sorry for my behavior. By following the program that has been laid out for me, I will do my best not to repeat the same behavior. I want you to know how sorry I am and to let me know how I can make this right."

This is the most you can do.

Some amends present special challenges. For instance, many alcoholics and addicts have financial issues when they get sober. This is something that I needed to address. I owed quite a bit of money to various people and had other debts I needed to pay back. And I was low on financial resources. When I first got sober, my earning capacity simply wasn't much. I was a cook by trade and not a very good one (ha, ha). Then, I started working with a man who was a gardener. I think I was making about $8.00 an hour.

I sat down with my sponsor, we looked at my financial amends, and we designed a plan to pay back all the money I owed. I know what you're thinking because I was thinking it, too: "I have so much debt, I can never pay it back." If you trust in this new power you've tapped into, and stay away from fear; if you take the direction and follow the 12-Step principles, amazing things will come to light. I keep saying it because it's true: you're now vibrating at a different level. If you are willing, wonderful things can and will happen.

It's never easy to make amends. The painful memories have to come up, as does the shame that comes with them. Some of us had criminal offenses we had to deal with, including the ones for which we were never caught. These must be addressed. They may be, at minimum, unpaid traffic or parking tickets. At the other end of the scale, are felonies and even more severe offenses. One thing we must continue to remind ourselves is that *we are getting our life in order*, cleaning up the wreckage of our past. *It's a process, not an event.* We cannot get this all done in one day or even one year. Remember that when we started this, we vowed and were willing to go to any lengths to get better.

When it comes to our financial amends, we assess each situation individually. We do what we can with the means we have. If we have several parking tickets or moving violations, we set up a time to speak to a public defender or an attorney to find out the best course of action to take. Most of the time, if you are showing some sort of effort to clean up the past, no judge will ignore that gesture.

Trickiest and most troubling for me were the amends for criminal harm. The fact was, I had several serious offenses for which I had not been caught. I had stolen several thousand dollars in larceny. Some of my offenses involved violence.

My sponsor's sensible directions were not to throw myself to the wolves. He suggested I come up with an amount of how much money I thought I had taken and find an agency or nonprofit I could contribute to—starting with making payments I could afford at that time. The program I found was Victims of Violent Crime. Working together, my sponsor and I figured out the approximate amount I owed for my thefts and I made monthly payments, until I paid it off. I like to think of this as a pay-it-forward example of cleaning up the past by doing things right in the present.

Like I said, every case is different. Please remember, when we sit down with someone who can give us an objective view, like our sponsor, we are able to see the bigger picture more clearly.

There is another category we look at in making amends: people to whom we owe amends who are no longer around or who have died. I had two or three people on my list who had passed away by the time I was making my amends. I had no idea where some of them were laid to rest. My sponsor's direction in this was to write a letter of amends and read it to him or her. Remember, Steps Eight and Nine are about the willingness to go to any lengths to make amends. I did know where a few of the deceased people on my list were buried, so for them, I wrote a letter and reviewed it with my sponsor. We then visited the cemetery together and I sat down and read the letter to them right there over their graves. These were very emotional yet freeing events in my life and I know there will be similar ones in yours.

The whole process of the amends, Steps Eight and Nine, feels remarkably cleansing. It will not always go your way as you revisit and repair the old and deep damage you caused. Some parties, like my uncle, won't accept your amends. But that does not matter, it's all part of the process. You need to stay connected to a loving, higher energy and do the work to live as your Highest Self. Knowing that you're willing to do the best that you can, continuing to work the principles of the program and take contrary action to your worst inclinations, as well as help others, is all you can do. And it is enough. Being mindful and conscientious in everything you do will illuminate your new path forward.

One more thing on the topic of making amends: making amends to ourselves. The biggest amends we make to ourselves is to not drink or use anymore. We are no longer hurting our bodies on a regular basis. Another amends we can do for ourselves is to actively work our spiritual programs. And, perhaps the best advice I've gotten about making amends is, *Don't beat yourself up.*

Beauty and healing happens in the Middle Six Steps. Now that we've concluded the Middle Steps, we have set ourselves up for the final Steps, Ten Through Twelve.

The Growth Steps

Step 10: Awareness
Step 11: Love
Step 12: Service

CHAPTER 6
The Growth Steps

———

Here we start the last three Steps.

Program members often group the 12 Steps into three parts of related steps: We call Steps One through Three, **The Acceptance Steps**; Four through Nine, **The Action Steps**; and Ten through Twelve, **The Growth Steps**. Some people like to call them the Maintenance Steps; I see them as the Growth Steps because they allow me to continue to grow by living according to a set of principles; ones that I want to keep transforming me into a more loving and compassionate human being. Continued growth in recovery is what we do to stay mentally and emotionally fit, so we can be of maximum service to ourselves and other human beings.

Step 10

"Continued to take personal inventory and when we were wrong, promptly admitted it."

We took our first inventory in Step Four, when we did a searching and moral—truth finding—inventory. We went on a truth finding-mission about ourselves. Here, we're asked to continue to look for resentments and fears, and to examine our conduct in all of our relationships. We continue to look for defects of character, for our own shortcomings, again because recovery is a process, not an event. When our defects do crop up, Step Ten directs us to again turn our thoughts inward. The goal, ultimately, is to be helpful to another human being; again, contrary action. Always remember, this is a work in progress. We practice for a lifetime.

As I've said, practice does not make perfect, practice *i s* perfect. The question is, what practical steps should we take to keep our personal inventory one of progress that helps others?

Some people like to write a daily inventory. They may keep journals or jot down reflections in the morning or before bed. While I was never a scribe who did a check and balance list on paper every day, I do think it can be helpful. I tended to examine things as they came up. But sometimes, I would let things build

Music is part of my recovery. There's nothing I love better than to sing my song. This is with my band at the Vu Doo Lounge, 2017.

up for a time and then I would have to write a whole inventory of resentments. Other times, I would write an inventory specifically on my fears, or write an inventory of my relationship conduct. I found when I focused on one inventory task at a time, I was better able to clarify my thoughts and feelings. Continuity is more important than frequency. At least that's the way it worked for me.

What happened to me in working this process—working a program, living by a new set of principles, doing contrary action—is that it became an almost organic working part of my life. At a certain point, when something came up, the process had become intuitive, and I naturally knew what course of action to take. This is what I mean by change. You are in the process of becoming a new person.

When Carl Jung talked about his interpretation of a spiritual awakening, he said, "Ideas, thoughts, and attitudes were set aside, and we're living by a new set of principles." (From the Big Book of AA, page 27.) As we change by working this new set of principles that connects us to positive energy, going back to drugs and alcohol does not even seem like it's in the equation anymore. It's literally *no longer an option* once this transformation has taken root. As we continue to strive for higher states of consciousness, we easily come to understanding, empathy, and forgiveness.

More than anything, Step Ten is the first growth step that reminds us that our continuing personal inventories are geared toward love and service. What can we give, not what can we take. Connecting with this higher energy, practicing these principles, this becomes a natural, integrated part of our life. We take inventory and when we are wrong, promptly admit it. This is how we free ourselves from fear, resentments, and self-harm.

Step 11

"Sought through prayer and meditation to improve our conscious contact with God as we understood Him, praying only for knowledge of His will for us and the power to carry that out."

I can guess what you're saying after reading this Step: "How on earth are you going to get us through this Step, Dave—it *says* God, *right there?*" Well, yes, it packs prayer, meditation and conscious contact with a force greater than ourselves. So, let us unpack this Step. Let's break it down, section by section.

Let us start with prayer. When I first got into the program I was told by other members of 12-Step groups, as well as my sponsor, that prayer was a way of being thankful, and of getting humble and small within the universe. I found that idea to be enormously helpful—that everyone can feel gratitude and humility. We have the capacity. What I mean by "humble and small" isn't putting ourselves down, it's knowing there's an energy out there that is so much greater than us. We can align ourselves with *this something that is bigger than us.* This power will support us completely in our recovery process. It's not about what we believe, it's about what we *experience.*

I had to think, when I prayed, who was I praying to, or what was I actually doing? My answer was that I basically aligned myself setting an intention with a force bigger than me—call it love. In my prayer or affirmation, I was committing to do the next right thing. I was also actively not wanting or not intending to go back to the life I had been living before. If this is something I needed to do, *I did it.* When I prayed, I would say something like this: "I thank the program, I thank my sponsor, I send loving thoughts to loved ones, as well as to my enemies. Help me align myself with this loving energy, give me the courage to take direction and to ensure my sobriety *one more day.*" It's basically my saying, *thank you*: thank you, I'm glad there is a program I can work with that will help me get over my addiction. I am grateful.

As time went on, I realized this isn't really a prayer, it is more an affirmation of my Intentions. I am affirming what I want. I am declaring *what I want to create*. It's kind of hard to create something without stating what it is you want, no? It's important to form intentions based on setting clear goals.

The idea that we can manifest what we envision is called the "law of attraction." First, we declare what it is we want. Identifying what that is changes our thought process by making it purposeful. That draws what we want toward us. I know that sometimes we can risk magical thinking about the future and also that we must be careful what we wish for! But there is definitely a power that comes from clearly identifying a goal and asking the universe to support it. I know because it's happened in my life.

One example came when I started a shampoo company about ten years ago with my then-wife. I really wanted our product to be distributed by Whole Foods Market but every time we approached them, we were met with massive resistance. They didn't like our labels, the price point was too high, on and on. One afternoon, I went into a Whole Foods store in Venice, California and took a photograph of the natural products section, specifically the shelves where they displayed all the shampoos. Back in my office, I used Photoshop to transpose the photograph of our products onto the photo I took in Whole Foods. I hung it up on my wall.

I looked at that photo every single day, envisioning our product placement there. Meanwhile, also every single day, I took action-steps towards achieving this goal, researching and networking and trying new avenues to sell our shampoo at Whole Foods. The day came when I met a distributor who had a connection there. After several meetings, Whole Foods introduced our products in their Southern California region, finally! They started to roll out our products. I was going around from store-to-store, training staff, thrilled that it was all finally happening. And, when I entered the store in El Segundo, I was blown away! It looked *exactly* like my vision board photo! I was moved to tears. All the energy had come together and definitively moved into alignment.

It took three years of envisioning, persistence and hard work. I always had this knowing that it was going to happen; I just didn't know when. It was a very spiritual moment for me. I felt an overwhelming sense of satisfaction and gratitude for the unfolding of the process. It was also a humbling moment. Even though I had a knowing in my heart, it still felt like a huge miracle. Like I was plugged into something much bigger than me.

I want to now turn to the "meditation" part of Step Eleven.

Meditation is amazing. In my early clean time, meditating for me was just about reading certain books written for 12-Step programs. For years, I read the Hazelden Twenty-Four Hours a Day book, and that was my meditation. Basically, I was trying to get some direction from a message that always seemed to address just how I was feeling that day. A lot of times I would read the day's message and say, "Wow, that is so on-point, that is exactly what I'm going through right now!" (And how many times have we had the experience in meetings that someone shares exactly what we need to hear in that moment? It's beautiful. That is so reassuring—to know that if you slip, it does not negate the work that you have done. There will always be a message that feels like it's meant for you. That's why we say, "Keep coming back.")

Meditation is an ongoing deal, part of the overall process of working the Steps. You're constantly refreshing yourself, learning and re-energizing to help others. The program is unique in that there's no finish line, there's no graduation. This is about growth toward continuously living a loving life, a kind life, a life free of alcohol and drugs. It is also about living with some sort of serenity and peace. In meditation practice, you can go as deep as you like.

As time went on, I wanted to move beyond reading 12-Step literature as meditation and learn how to meditate properly. There are tons of tutorials online and apps for guided meditation to help you at any stage of meditation. I also read books on the subject and talked to people who were versed in it.

I was really interested in Vipassana meditation, where people sit silently for ten days and focus only on the breath. I explored Zen meditation, as well as a lot of guided meditation. When I first started meditating, I thought, "This is silly. All I'm doing is sitting here thinking." What I learned over time, though, was to let my thoughts come and go without judgment. It's part of my daily practice and helps me to find some peace and settle down a little bit.

I have a ritual that I do every morning before I meditate. I align myself with a loving energy and set an intention. I thank the people in the program who have helped me. I thank the program. I write out a gratitude list, which can be quite diverse, ranging from my daughter, Maya, to the Stoic philosophers Seneca and Marcus Aurelius. I read four different spiritual books, not only from 12-Step programs, but all different kinds of literature. A lot of the books have the words God or spirit in them. Just as you will use whatever word resonates with you, I always replace the word *God*, with love or the *universe* or with the *program*. Each day, I sit in silent meditation for twenty to thirty minutes, but it took me years to get to this place.

I think about my days in early sobriety when all I could think of to say was, "Thank you," as a version of a prayer, and read the *Twenty-Four Hours a Day* book as my meditation. But even by just doing that, I felt gently led into wanting to take my practice deeper. As I said, there was no place to get to. I could go at my own pace. That's true for everyone on this path. It continues to amaze me today, thirty years into it, that we can continue to grow and become the person we always wanted to be or, rather, uncover who we have actually always been. We are clearing away the parts of us that are not authentic, not who we really are, so that we can be our higher selves or the best version of our selves.

The last part of Step Eleven says, "…Praying only for knowledge of His will for us and the power to carry that out."

I like to break this part of the step into two parts. The first part means you're listening and the second part means you're doing what you're advised to do.

His "will," in my interpretation, simply means *following the program*. And then taking the action steps to carry out its directions. My "self-will" says, "I do not need to do these things." (Things like go to a meeting, listen to my sponsor or make commitments at meetings.) The will of the program is that I do these things, that I take contrary action, to what my head or "self" might be telling me.

We align ourselves with the principles of the program, not our self-will. We are taking this contrary action and doing something that may feel unnatural. But taking contrary action gives you the "power to carry it out." You are empowering yourself by doing something you would not do on your own.

We must push ourselves and get help from our community of other people in recovery. Talk with your sponsor, do whatever you need to do to take the appropriate actions. Get up and do the next right thing. We are all on this path together, we pull ourselves together, not alone. Keep taking action, every day it will come to you. You will start to feel different, you will want to help other people get the gift you have been given. You will not have to preach. People will start to see the change in you, the light in your eyes, and the transformation in your attitude. This is a program of attraction, not promotion. People will now be attracted to your energy.

It works, it really does. You can do this, and the wonderful part is you do not have to do it alone. You are co-creating a spiritual awakening for yourself and in your community with your fellow brothers and sisters in sobriety who are walking this path with you.

Step 12

"Having had a spiritual awakening as the result of these Steps, we tried to carry this message to alcoholics, and to practice these principles in all our affairs."

So here we are at Step Twelve, which, like Step Eleven, can be broken down into three parts. The three parts of Step 12 are:

1) Spiritually awakening

2) Carrying the message to addicts and alcoholics

3) Practicing these principles in all our affairs

A spiritual awakening is a shift in perception. You see things in a different light.

The spiritual awakening in Step Twelve comes about in our attitude, ideas, and emotions by taking the previous eleven Steps. As we take the actions of each one of those Steps, we begin to align ourselves with a new and different energy. The metamorphosis is already well underway. We will be relieved of the insanity of addiction, and in the process, we begin to wake up. This is where you start to experience synergy on a regular basis in your life.

Synchronicities happen more and more as you start to pay attention. Synchronicities are seemingly coincidental events. As you continue to work with other alcoholics/addicts and to give yourself over to self-less service in action, you will be amazed at what will start to take root in your life. Coincidences do not seem to be coincidental. Things happen that naturally seem to mesh.

Self-less service in action is a cornerstone of the program. People sacrifice their personal time for the newcomer. They are willing to give their time and energy to care and help newbies understand the process. When I first met my sponsor, I was still locked up in the state penitentiary, and here was a man who stepped away from his family and life and took the time to drive, go through prison security, and spend countless hours with me on the visiting yard. All for a young man trying to navigate the 12 Steps. This is a great example of someone caring enough to carry the message to another alcoholic. I am forever indebted to him. As you'll discover, it's the greatest feeling in the world to be able to pay it forward.

When you reach Step Twelve, you've plowed the fertile soil of the garden called your life, and some healthy fruits have started to grow. You have calmed down quite a bit by now. Peace and serenity have become more the norm these days in your everyday experience.

Remember that Step Ten tells us that sanity has returned. Sanity is a wholeness of mind. Imagine being able to process a cognitive thought or make a rational decision in the context of alcoholism. When the obsession has been lifted, you feel the energy shift. You're aligned with a new "program for living." This is not magical, this is a practical application of the program.

Enjoying a meal at my hometown favorite, the Natural Café
in Santa Barbara, California. 2018.

Until you've been helped by a fellow addict, it's hard to conceive of trusting so wholly in someone who has gone through the process before you. It's especially hard not to question them and simply believe that if you do this, it will work. For an infinite number of other people and for me, it has worked.

I think of the time I went to an attorney to formulate a plan for a business deal. He gave me an eight-point plan to use. He said, "If you follow this plan to a tee, it will most likely work." He asked me to trust him and take the appropriate action. I chose to have faith in him because this was his area of expertise. I followed the plan and, sure enough, it worked! I got the result I wanted by going to an expert, someone who had gone down the road before me. Just like someone guiding you through the 12 Steps.

So, having had a spiritual awakening, you are now aligning yourself in a distinctly better energy field. You are vibrating on a different level, walking in the light and no longer in the darkness. I'm so happy there is no graduation in 12-Step programs. The program's ongoing nature means that we always have the opportunity to continue to grow and take this as far as we'd like to go. It's now your time to pay it forward. This takes us to part two of the Twelfth Step: "Carry this message to alcoholics and addicts."

Now it's time to pass on what we've been given. You will be able to share with them what happened in your own case by working the 12 Steps. The energy you feel is reciprocal—you cannot keep it unless you give it away. That is why you see people with a lot of time in the program still showing up at meetings and working with newcomers. Yes, service is also for their own recovery, but if the "old-timers" were not in meetings, there would be no one there to help those who have less experience. It's one of the oldest spiritual laws in every culture; the elders pass on the wisdom to the younger ones. In our cases, it's not so much younger as measured in years, but in sobriety time.

I still continue to work with newcomers, I still go to meetings and I also still have a sponsor. I get the greatest feeling in the world when working with someone new. It's when I feel the most serenity and love. I actually love giving something away and not wanting anything in return. Watching the lights come on in someone's eyes, seeing their obsession lift and them living a loving and productive life—there's nothing better. I have worked with many newcomers over the years. It has been the greatest gift, it keeps the good energy flowing.

Some people in the program have told me that they do not feel like they have anything to give. They're not sure if they're doing it right. I wasn't sure if I was doing it right, either. I just did the exact same thing as the person who showed *me* how to do it. Carrying the message can mean a lot of things: taking someone to a meeting, talking to a newcomer, or being an example of how this program works. If we get stuck, we do it together. We can always lean on each other. One of my favorite program sayings is, "I can't, we can."

One of my more challenging years was 1996. I had been sober for almost seven years. Then a major confluence of events occurred in my life. It was like a trifecta of altered realities: my mother's death, buying a new home, and changing careers. It was exciting and frightening at the same time. Each of these events scores high on the list of major life stressors and can produce enough anxiety and heightened emotion to keep you agitated for days on end. (Meditation!) To experience them all in the same year was epic.

Six and a half years sober, I was working at Klein Bottle as a drug and alcohol counselor for high-risk youth. Just after the first of the year, an ex-boss told me about the job at the sheriff's department designing and implementing a drug and alcohol treatment program for inmates in the county jail. That's the job I never thought I could get or even apply for with my past criminal history. He encouraged me to go ahead anyway. I turned in my application on February 14,

1996. As I wrote earlier, I *did* get that job, which still amazes me, but until the day I heard, "You're hired," I was preoccupied with the uncertainty, suspense and fear. (And longing. I *really* wanted that job.)

At the same time, my then-wife and I were looking for a commercial/residential piece of property to live and run a day spa out of. It was becoming problematic and stressful because there were no lots available in Santa Barbara at that time. We ended up finding a place in Summerland, California, a short distance away. The property came with an old abandoned dog kennel and an 800-square-foot California bungalow that would be our home. We put an offer on the property in May.

By then, my parents had moved to Fresno to look after my grandmother, who was in her 90s. I received a call one night in late May; my grandmother was in the hospital with heart failure. Obviously, I was concerned and upset and let my family know that if there was anything I could do, I would be there immediately. Because my mother and father were there to look after her, I didn't have to drive up immediately. But the very next day, my sister Darline called me and said, "Mom's in the hospital." I said, "No, Grandma's in the hospital." And she said, "They're both in the hospital now. Something's wrong with mom's blood." My mother had a nosebleed that wouldn't stop. My sister asked me to get to Fresno as soon as I could.

The next day I took off work and drove the four hours from Santa Barbara to Fresno. It was strange when I arrived at the hospital; my grandmother was on one floor and my mother was on another. My mother didn't seem sick, just a little tired. My father was very anxious and worried. I went with my sisters Darity and Darline to a sit-down meeting with the doctor, who explained my mother's condition. He told us that she had leukemia, the progressive blood cancer, and that she had about six months to live. We were all shocked. This came out of seemingly nowhere. My father had been the one dealing with poor health issues for the past dozen years, ever since his stroke in 1984. My mother had been the healthy parent.

We tried to absorb the blow. There is something that happens to you physically when you're told devastating news. It's almost surreal. I felt sick to my stomach, overwhelmed with a feeling of impending loss for my mother. We all think we will live forever, or that it will never happen to us until it does. Losing a parent at any age is like losing a part of yourself. My mind was too overloaded to think clearly about what this would mean; we let the doctor's words sink in. None of us siblings wanted to believe what was happening. We didn't know what to say.

First, we had to tell my father.

My mother was his world. As dysfunctional as their relationship was, I believe my dad loved her in his own capacity. They had been married for about forty-five years at that point.

My sisters and I walked out of the meeting into the hallway where my father waited. He could tell by the look on our faces that something was very wrong. I tried to play it off for a minute but he kept pressuring us to tell him what was going on so we took him into a quiet room and broke the news. I think it was my sister Darity who actually said the words, "Mom has six months to live." I only saw my father cry a few times in my life and this was one of them. I was grateful to be there to comfort him, and let him know that we were here as a family.

The next couple of days were interesting and not what I would have expected. My conversations with my mom were really amazing in their depth and raw honesty. My clearest memory of those days was how close I felt to her as we connected on a deeper level. My mother was not only my mother; she was a fellow member of Alcoholics Anonymous. The power of that was so moving to me. I felt like I would never forget the conversations we were having in that time. And I never have. It spanned the sublime to the ridiculous; at one point, she looked at me and said, "I'm not gonna buy any green bananas."

She told me that she did not want to die in Fresno. My sister Darline agreed to have her at her home in Harbor City. My mom had always been very active in her recovery program in the South Bay area of Los Angeles. She had sponsored so many women and there was a lot of love for her there. This is one of the great things about the program, the camaraderie in the fellowship; people are always willing to help.

Six of my friends and I rented a U-Haul truck and moved my mother to Harbor City. She didn't look sick, just really tired and weak. In the next two weeks after we re-located her, she attended meetings with my sister and my then-wife, made dinners and lived pretty much as she normally would. But in the two weeks after that, she took a turn for the worse. It was pretty traumatizing for everyone. We'd already contacted hospice care and now they were coming in to care for her (and us). I had no idea things would go so fast. Her body began to deteriorate; she could no longer get out of bed. My sisters and I would take care of her and sit next to her bed.

My mother and I had some great conversations in her last weeks. We talked about everything from her growing up to how happy she was that I was sober. We had deep talks about religion, my belief system, her belief system. One thing about my mom is that she would never judge me or what other people believe. She was very passionate and committed to her own religious beliefs. She was a devout Christian and she would tell me that she was ready to go home to Jesus. She had decided that she didn't want to go through any of the gnarly treatment that was offered. She knew it was her time and she wasn't going to fight it.

My mother hadn't smoked in years, but one day she asked me if I would get her a cigarette. Everyone else was freaking out, saying that she couldn't smoke. I got her the cigarette she wanted—what difference would it make at that point?—and she could barely take a hit but she did and that was it, that was what she wanted. Her body was failing, her eyes were swollen, she was getting sores all over her body. It is so hard to watch your mother go through so much pain. I remember walking down the stairs with my sister, and her saying, "God, this is so hard to see her that way, I need a drink." I was thinking to myself, "I need a drink, myself, *but I don't drink.* I have to go through this process completely awake, with nothing to numb this pain."

I can only tell you from my experience that something definitely happened to me during this time helping my mother die. It was a spiritual experience. To be completely present feeling every emotion, good and bad, was definitely a growing experience. I don't want to say I became a better man, but I did have a breakthrough and looked at life through a new set of glasses.

I remember one instance when hospice sent me to the hospital to pick up my mother's medication. When I got to the pharmacy, the pharmacist slid over a bottle of pure morphine. It was like time stopped and I was in the Twilight Zone. As he slid the vial over to me with her other medication, I thought for a moment that there was a time in my life where I would have gone through a brick wall with a spoon to get to a vial of morphine. But my perception had changed by working a program. This design for living brought about a psychic change in me. I didn't think twice about that vial; the medication was only there for my mother to help her with her pain.

In those two weeks before she died, I was there to help support my father and, especially, to sit with my mother for hours on end. I was the baby of the family and my mother loved me dearly, unconditionally. There were times when I was talking to her and her eyes were so swollen that I put wet wash cloths on them to help with the swelling. I would ask her, "Mom can you see me?" She would respond with, "I'll never forget how sweet your face is." I would hold back the tears knowing I wanted to be there for my mother in that moment; I would cry later in private. She asked me if I would write her eulogy, and deliver it at her funeral. She asked me to promise a couple of other things, too. One was to take care of my father. She said I was the only one of the children who could do it. My dad was a handful then. I agreed.

I was so blown away by the level of support that my mom had in her community of sober women. Every day, a different woman would come and bring the family all three meals. They never asked to come in and see my mom; they were there to support her during these times and that meant supporting all of us. You could feel the power of their kindness.

My mom and I laughed and cried. I was able to be present for my mom, because I was sober, because I was awake. Things were so different when I was drinking and using. I could never be present for anyone; it was always about me and my self-centered behavior. The 12 Steps teach us to go outside of ourselves and be there for other people, not wanting anything in return. Love and service is our code. Being present for me also meant that when my mother died, we were current. There was nothing left to work out, no unfinished business. I was a changed human through that experience. I can now understand, have empathy, and compassion for someone who's going through the same thing with a loved one.

My mother died in the afternoon of June 30, 1996. Her spirit lives forever. A week later, on July 8th, I turned seven years sober. I bought the house, and got the job with the Santa Barbara County Sheriff's Department. What a year!

Three huge life's events. And the whole time, I felt supported by the program. I was not living by fear. I would get up and do the next right thing. I would act my way into the right thinking. By taking the appropriate action, we are on the right path and I truly felt the impact of that in the spring and summer of 1996.

My mom's funeral was truly a celebration of her life. What seemed to be a thousand people came to honor her; just a few of the countless lives she had touched through her program. My nephew and friends of mine who were close to my mom were pallbearers at her funeral. My mother died not with a fortune of money, but with a wealth of love. I inherited all her spiritual and recovery books. I still have her 27-year AA chip. I still end my meditation every day smiling and thanking her for my life and the time that we spent together.

Love you, Mom.

We all go through some difficult times in life, even during the progress of recovery. There are deaths in the family. Financial setbacks. Relationship issues. This is just life. It happens whether we're sober or not. Everyone must cope with life's stresses and losses. I've gone through it all in the last thirty years. You name it: death, divorce, job changes, financial anxiety. How do we absorb the initial shocks and keep on a steady, healthy course?

What I've learned more than anything is how my reaction or response to certain situations affects how they are resolved. I have fallen short at times. But everything can be a positive learning experience when alcohol or drugs is not your default mode. You get stronger each time as you mature both emotionally and spiritually. And you constantly have to remind yourself that it doesn't happen all at once; it's a process.

Newcomers sometimes ask me, "How do I live one day at a time and still maintain some hold on financial security, housing... you know, the basic living stuff, stuff that needs *planning*?"

"One day at a time" does not contradict the need for planning and self-care. But there is no need to go into panic mode when you feel you're falling below your comfort level. Getting through tough times calls all your program practice (and confidence in synergy) into play. It means doing the necessary footwork to do the next right thing, trusting the universe or however you conceive the larger context you operate in, and doing all you *can* do. For me, one of the best things that shifts my perspective is practicing Step 12; specifically, working with another alcoholic. Helping them to achieve sobriety gets me out of my head. Those are moments of pure bliss when I know this is my primary purpose and my other concerns are helping me serve it.

People who I don't even know come up to me at meetings and tell me, "I know you're going through hard times. I just want to let you know that it gives me hope to know you can go through anything, without drinking or using. Now I know I can go through something challenging and have dignity and respect like you do. Thank you for being a positive example." Being on the receiving end of that gift feels great. It feels even greater to give it.

Sharing the experience, strength and hope you've gained in the program is how you practice Step Twelve's affirmation to "carry the message." Whatever you do, remember love and service is our code. People go to meetings to stay connected, to be helped and to help other people.

I've worked with a lot of people. Some have stayed clean and sober, and some have died from this disease. Sadly, some just never get it. The best tools you have for sobriety are group support and working closely with a sponsor. I will always continue to put my hand out there to help another person find the way, feel the synergy, and vibrate at a different level. To practice love, compassion, forgiveness, and to be helpful is my only goal.

The great Indian yogi, Paramahansa Yogananda, who is often called the "Father of yoga in the West, has said, "*A person that has reformed has the capacity to reform thousands.*" Now you are equipped to help another human being, to carry the message. By doing this, you will keep the flow going of this higher vibrational energy that goes from you to others, into the world and beyond that, out to the universe.

This takes us to the last part of Step Twelve, "practice these principles in all of our affairs." Now that we have shifted our ideas, attitudes, and emotions into a positive energy field, it is easy to follow the principles of the program.

The specific principles we practice, Step by Step, are:

Step 1 – Honesty

Step 2 – Hope

Step 3 – Faith

Step 4 – Courage

Step 5 – Integrity

Step 6 – Willingness

Step 7 – Humility

Step 8 – Brotherly Love

Step 9 – Justice

Step 10 – Perseverance

Step 11 – Spirituality

Step 12 – Service

If you examine each one of these principles separately and try to live your life by practicing them collectively in all your affairs, you will be in a better place than you ever have been. You have traded the roller coaster highs and lows, its crawls and plunges, of your addiction for steady contentment and peace of mind. You will have to work at it every day, one day at a time. The road does get narrower—the highs and lows do even out. There was a time that

I never thought I would be able to wait twenty-four hours to react to emotional stresses.

When I say that practice does not *make* perfect, practice *is* perfect, I mean that we can never *do* anything perfectly, we can only *strive* for perfection. If we examine each situation where we are put to the test, whether it's at work, in your relationships, family issues, money, business dealings, how we interact with other people; when we apply the principles each time, we will have a better outcome. While doing the right thing doesn't always stave off disappointment or hurt—we can't make our partners love us, we can't close every deal, we can't be perfect parents or children—it can help us set an example for others. This is what we can do by consistently "practicing these principles in all our affairs."

If we set our goals on living by this set of principles, by doing contrary action to our old ways and compulsions, our lives get better in unimaginable ways. Do the footwork and then relinquish your attachment to the outcome. That may be the hardest work of all because we are trained from childhood to focus on outcomes. We're taught that games are for winning, relationships are for living happily ever after, and money reflects our worth.

But when we shift the energy in and around us into a positive, loving, compassionate, higher vibrational energy, the grasp for outcomes falls away. That's when you enjoy simply playing a game, delighting in another person, and letting go of the idea that money has anything at all to do with your value. It may sound kind of airy-fairy, but the point is that now you're living in a higher vibrational field. That loosens your attachment to outcomes. It frees you in so many ways.

There are two emotions that drive our lives: one is fear, the other is love. If you look at every decision you make in life, it's coming from one of these two places, fear or love. It's a choice. You can shift this energy to being loving instead of fearful. The choice is yours.

By now, you have really put in the work going through all of the 12 Steps. And, look you did it, without necessarily using the word God! There is room in the program for *every* alcoholic and addict.

It's important to always remember that this is a lifelong process. If you are diligent about the choices you make in your daily life, good things will come to pass and you will perceive that you have a wonderful life, maybe one that's now beyond your wildest imagination. It's not going to be all rainbows and unicorns, but you'll know how to deal with the peaks as well as the valleys. You've empowered yourself.

Maybe you can't see all of the gifts unfolding in your life right away, but others can and they will see the spark of transformation within you. They call it slow-briety for a reason. There will come a time when you look around at the outer circumstances of your life, the healed relationships, the new jobs, how you now react to circumstances that used to baffle or enrage you, and see it all with insight and clarity. And the biggest thing is, you're no longer obsessed with drinking or using. You're healthier, you're treating yourself more kindly, you are giving and receiving love.

You have had a spiritual awakening as a result of the Steps. Your life is changing slowly but surely. You have peeled away the layers of the onion to get to know your truest self, a person that comes from compassion and wants to be helpful to their fellow human beings. You embody how the Dalai Lama defines compassion in his book, The Compassionate Life:

"Compassion is the wish for another human being to be free from suffering. Love is wanting them to have happiness."

AFTERWORD

SUSANVILLE, CALIFORNIA 1986

When you get sober, the time of your active disease seems like another life. You feel wonder and gratitude that you almost don't recognize yourself anymore in what now seems like a horror movie. But you don't forget what happened. As painful as it is for me to remember things that happened when I was so messed up as an addict, I do take some pride that my brain is now clear enough to remember every detail of that pain. My story—and yours—is what we bring to our service to others. Our stories connect our community.

My most vivid, humiliating pain (and it's hard to choose when every part of your life made you feel shame) comes from lock-up. Some young people go from middle school to high school to college. I went from juvenile hall to county jail to state prison. All my life's "undergraduate" prison experiences in L.A. was to get me ready for California's Correctional Center in Susanville. By then, I had a pretty good idea of how to "program." ("Program" in this context means how to conduct yourself when doing time.)

Susanville actually has two state prisons, the California Correctional Center, which is designated a minimal-medium security facility, and the newer High Desert State Prison. (Not to be confused with a same-name prison in Nevada.) About twenty years ago, a federal correctional institution opened in Herblong, California, about forty miles to the east. The impact of the prisons on the town of Susanville is huge. With a population of less than 20,000—including more than 6,000 inmates—in 2007, nearly half the town's adult population works in the prisons. (Susanville was the subject of a documentary that year, *Prison Town, USA,* that aired on PBS.)

The town needed the jobs. Once a hub of lumber, mining, and farming, Susanville largely lost these industries as they changed or slowed down. In fact, the only growth industry there in the last fifty-five or so years has been prison. Susanville's correctional facilities are located the furthest north in the California prison system. They get a lot of inmates but not a lot of visitors.

I served my first state prison time there in 1986-1987. First I had to be "processed," and the association of that word with lunch meat isn't far off. Everybody has to go through the same series of intake procedures to be officially in the joint. I was processed through Chino, east of L.A., the jail I saw my dad in, which processed all prisoners in Southern California.

By then I'd noticed that being in jail had already changed how I behaved there. Prison makes you get used to things that you would never get used to living on the streets. The way you live in such small quarters and have to get comfortable going to the bathroom in front of other people. Group showering, segregated eating, depending on race, alliances, or gangs. You develop an inner guard that tells you that everything and everyone is suspect, and I mean *everyone*; guards, convicts, *everyone*. You have to be on your game at all times.

Getting processed for Susanville started with a psych evaluation in Chino. Then they assigned me a level of custody security and determined the appropriate prison. The prison system in California uses a point tally. Based on your number of points, you're categorized as Level One or low custody, which means minimum security, or fire camp. (Fire camp is a state corrections program that allows non-violent, minimum security inmates to train as fire fighters in camps for that purpose.) Level Two custody is a medium-secured prison that has dorms. In Level Three, you live in a cell, not a dorm. Level Four gets you cell living with less accommodations. Level Five, the highest custody, is considered lockdown or "the hole."

Level One prisoners have the most freedom, working outside the walls, training to be firefighters. You get more yard time. You're not locked up as much. Level Two prisoners are not allowed to go outside the walls to work for the prison or go to fire camp. Level Three means you're locked up in your cell a lot more and you have no freedoms outside the walls.

To my relief, in Chino, I was evaluated as a Level One with minimum custody. I was a drug dealer with no gang affiliation and not too long a history as a violent criminal. So, when I learned I'd be shipped to Susanville, with its three levels of prison yards, I expected to do my time there training as a hotshot firefighter.

California always transports prisoners at night. The night I left Chino, I remember that I was extremely nervous and frightened, but I couldn't show any signs of that. That was tough; the feeling I got in my stomach is that I wanted to throw up from the nerves. And I knew just where the nerves came from. The word in the yard was that Susanville was rioting a lot. Because its location discouraged visitors, there weren't a lot of drugs on their yards. At the time, drugs primarily came in through visitors. When there are more drugs on the yard, inmates are happier, obviously. (Only a drug addict would think this situation was "obvious." But it was always calmer with drugs and the tension ratcheted up without them.) I remember sitting on the bus thinking to myself, "There's no way to get out of this. I'd better man up or there'll be big problems for me up there."

The bus left Chino at 3 o'clock in the morning. I was shackled for the long 15-hour bus ride. My senses were freaking out: I heard the sounds of chains mixed with the sounds of laughter. The bus smelled like a rotten dairy farm. The prison that you're leaving always has a buzz to it; you can hear it, you can smell it. It felt profoundly disturbing to me *not to have a choice*, to know you're driving straight into hell and you have to act as if it's all good.

That's what I remember about riding up Highway 395 on the backside of the Sierras, shackled and chained. Soon there were more sounds: the tires on the road, people snoring. The mixture of smells: body odor and cheap cologne. (Only the officers wore cologne.)

There are always three correctional officers on the bus transporting you to another prison. I looked around, matching the officers' faces with names I thought up. There was a white guy who I called Clint Eastwood (not to his face of course), a black guy who became Shaft, and a Mexican guy I started thinking of as Poncho Villa. These guys were fucking serious. They wore full bulletproof vests and riot jumpsuits. They were armed to the teeth. One was holding a shotgun in the rear of the bus. One drove the bus; the third officer rode shotgun holding a mini .14 rifle.

The bus ride was long and hard. I always have a hard time sleeping on buses, trains or planes, even under the best of circumstances. I rested my head on the window, just looking around. Some people were sleeping, one was weeping and many others just stared into nowhere, no one knowing what fate would bring.

When the bus finally pulled up to Susanville in the late afternoon for R&R (receiving and release) processing, the scene was just what I expected. The prisoners already doing time there crowded at the yard fence to see who was arriving. White, black and Mexican inmates checked everybody out. They were there to see if friends or enemies were coming, or if someone needed to be harmed. You didn't know who among them had word of who was coming, a friend or foe, someone with information or a rat. I was surprised right away that two of my bus mates who I thought were the baddest guys on the bus looked at the inmates in the yard and went straight to an officer when they got off and asked to be put into protective custody. You never know what's going to happen in prison: trust no one. I once saw the littlest guy in jail—something must have happened to him; he was small, so probably rape— drop a 30-pound weight from the weight pile in the yard on top of the head of the baddest guy in prison. One of them went to the hospital; the other was never seen again.

Everyone Is suspect. *Everyone.*

Processing the new arrivals started on the Level Three yard. You'd be moved later if you'd been assigned Level One or Two, as I'd been, but everyone started here. I knew I might stay there in a cell for a few days or maybe a week before there was a Level One dorm bed for me. I wasn't concerned about it.

What I hadn't taken into account was that it wasn't only the new prisoners in the Level Three building. There were also Level Three convicts already doing their entire time there. Me, I was a Level One inmate eligible for fire camp.

I wasn't there forty-eight hours when the cold reality of California's prison system landed a gut punch.

It was my second day on the yard. I ran into a couple of guys I knew from Long Beach that I'd done time with in the L.A. County Jail. They explained to me that there was an issue with one of the opposing gangs and that we needed to take care of business. (I thought, "We?" But that's prison: you prove your loyalty. "No" isn't an option.) Somebody had burned someone for drugs. It was whites vs. blacks.

They told me that the plan was, fifteen minutes before yard recall, the white guys, including me, would attack the black gang. I remember the feeling of "*Oh FUCK, are you kidding me?*" But I couldn't show any signs of fear or not wanting to participate. That's the code of conduct within the prison population: you ride with us, or you ride against us. If I said that I didn't want anything to do with this, I would put my life in jeopardy. Fear and adrenaline raced through my veins. I didn't know exactly what to do—I saw guys holding knives in their hands; I had nothing but my fists.

When the shot caller gave the signal, the stabbings started. I hit the first black guy I saw. I felt someone jump on top of me and as he knocked me to the ground, I was throwing my fist not knowing if I was hitting anything. I heard gunshots. I smelled tear gas. How had I ended up in a prison riot from surfing and selling drugs on the beach? Over the PA system they yelled, "Everybody on the ground! Don't move or you will be shot!" There was dirt on my face. Blood gushed out of my nose. I guess I was hit. I saw one of the white guys start running towards an opposing gang member. A guard promptly shot him, wounding his stomach. I'm not sure what happened to him after that.

It must have taken the rest of the day and all night to book us into Administrative Segregation, a/k/a The Hole. *Great,* I said to myself. *Now I'm in prison in prison.*

There went fire camp.

There were about 60 of us in the hole, two of us to a cell. My cellmate was called Spongy because he had weird, frizzy ginger hair. He was little but his spongy-looking hair was big. He was a young, hot-headed kid from a part of San Bernardino known as "felony flats." No clothes were allowed in the hole, all we had on was our boxers. We had no mattresses for the first couple of days. The noise there was so deafening, I stuffed toilet paper in my ears to muffle the abusive yelling that went on all night. We got a shower once a week, escorted by guards. Another guard in the control tower across the way held a gun on us while we were in the shower. Trust me, you didn't want to make any sudden moves.

After a prison riot (or other infraction), you need to go to sergeants' court or, as I already knew from my other incarcerations, kangaroo court. They find you guilty of whatever it is, then take time away from you or increase your security risk. Both happened to me. I had arrived in Susanville as a Level One, minimum security; after the riot, I was a Level Three high-risk inmate.

What was more frightening to me than losing my minimum custody classification was that I knew immediately that the sergeant was going to play a game with me. He knew I had no gang affiliation. He told me that if I didn't start talking and tell him who instructed me to fight, I would be the only one out of the sixty people in the hole that he'd release. Then all of my homeboys would think I was a rat. That was a death sentence and he knew it.

No way was I breaking the inmate code of silence. I needed to take my chances that once the sergeant realized that his game wasn't working and he'd get nothing from me, he'd eventually send me back to my cell. I tried to be the face of courage while the little kid inside me felt so scared.

I was thinking ahead about that, actually. I was leery of telling Spongy what happened because, again, everyone is a suspect or possible spy against you, even your cellie. So I kept to myself. I had no idea when they would release me and put a rat jacket on me. This may explain why it took me such a long time when I got out of prison to have trust for normal people in the world. I couldn't quite get that they weren't all out to get me.

Two days went by and nothing happened. In fact, they never intended to live up to their promise of letting me out. I spent thirty-seven days in the hole. Now I was Level Three custody. And I was glad because something shifted in my psyche in that time.

In one way, I earned my prison stripes—I didn't give into the pressure, now I was one of them, I was respected and I survived. But a new feeling was starting to grow in me. I didn't like the way this experience felt. I didn't want to live this way forever. I wanted the shame and humiliation that I was used to feeling just living my life to be DONE.

In Susanville, I had something, something in my mind whispering that this wasn't going to be me forever. I knew then that something had to change. I didn't know what. I just knew someday, sometime, life would be different. And it is.

But I didn't really know that yet, not even when they let me out of Susanville on parole in 1988. They give you $200 when you get out. I had that and a pair of jeans that one of my sisters sent me. I was faced with the reality of how the world now saw me, on the hour-long plane ride from Reno to LAX. As I boarded the flight with a paper bag holding my stuff and found my aisle seat, I noticed the woman sitting in the middle seat and her young daughter, who was in the window seat. The mom looked at me and put her arm around her daughter. It was *me*. She was afraid for her daughter. They were scared of me. That was hard to process. But that was the way it would be for me for a long time to come.

I was trying to stay sober at the time. I stayed with my mom and went to a couple of meetings. I slipped after seeing my first sponsor at a meeting head for the pay phone, looking disheveled. This was the same man who used to bang on my door and yell, "STAY SOBER!" Seeing him this way was a shock. I didn't re-connect with him. Instead, I fell off the wagon.

Just as I was thinking of heading to San Diego to do bank robberies to keep me high on hard drugs, my cousin convinced me to go to my grandmother's. That's when I ended up in Fresno the time I tried to kick heroin—and failed, including the bank robbery with my female companion. The street lawyer my father found made a deal; three years. They brought me down to a Level One, which meant spending the last year of that sentence in fire camp. That's where I had my last shot of heroin, in 1989. July 8, 1989 was my sobriety date. A year later, with one year of sobriety, I was paroled.

The synchronicity of what happened next still moves me. On parole, I lived at one of Santa Barbara's oldest transition houses,

Newhouse Sober Living, which was founded in 1955, the year I was born. In the 90s, I managed the facility and served on its Criminal Justice Advisory Board—with my parole officer. Today, I am on its Board of Directors.

SANTA BARBARA, CALIFORNIA 2020

I am often asked by people new to 12-Step programs, "When do you think it will be time for me to leave the sober living house?" My answer is always the same: "When nothing changes except where you lay your head."

I tell them what I've tried to stress to you in this book: there is no finish line to cross or finals to take. Working the program is about getting up every day and doing the next right thing. The Steps give you every tool to do this. *The choice is yours.* You now have the information and the knowledge. Examine the decisions you make in life and ask yourself this: "*Will the decision I'm making right now affect the person that I'm dealing with in a positive or negative way? Will this affect me in a positive or negative way?*" Put the other person first while taking care of yourself, too. When you conduct your life with this non-selfish perspective to inform your behavior, things get better; it is inevitable, and that's true whether or not you're in a 12-Step program.

We've talked a lot about connecting with a power greater than ourselves, which is part of the solution to our alcoholism or other addiction. We've talked about having a spiritual remedy that treats our disease. Change the behavior, do the contrary action, come from a loving compassionate place, do the work that it takes to change *your* perspective, nobody else's. When you do this, you cannot help but connect with the synergy.

Knowing you're willing to do the best that you can, continuing to work the principles of the program, continuing to take contrary action, and helping others, is all you can do. Being mindful and conscientious in everything you do starts to illuminate a new path in your life.

You are not alone. Everyone in recovery has done these things. Stay out of the guilt and remorse; you are designing your life *now*. What has happened to you before sobriety is actually an asset in that it allows you to take your experience and use it to help other people. When I start slipping into worry and remorse, I remember one thing: everything seems to work itself out. Stay in the moment because the moment is all we have. I always remember, if I get up and do the next right thing, if I do not drink or use, if I work the program, things will get better. And they do.

Love yourself, you're worth it.

I want to thank each and every one of you for reading this book. If I've helped one person, I've done my job. My life has truly changed for the better by doing the things outlined in these pages. I am now living a life beyond my wildest dreams. Again, thank you so much for taking the time. I'm here, cheering you on.

Love and Light,

David

ABOUT THE AUTHOR

Thirty years ago, David Vartabedian was an alcoholic, drug addict and criminal who was in and out of the California prison and parole system from ages 13 to 33. After several false starts at sobriety, he embraced 12-Step programs in the last year of a three-year sentence for armed robbery. He has been clean and sober since 1989.

After his release, he studied psychology at Santa Barbara City College and worked as a laborer. From there, he became the assistant manager and then manager at the sober living house where he had transitioned back into the community. His career as a youth substance abuse counselor included running a program for high-risk teenagers in Santa Barbara. Then the County Sheriff's Department hired him to design and implement a treatment education program for county inmates, working with California's Drug Court diversion program.

Though he first believed that his record as a felon would bar him from working in the county correctional system, its officials became his advocates. His innovative recovery treatment program was so successful, he became a board member of the Santa Barbara County Criminal Justice Advisory Board and the National Council on Alcoholism.

Currently, he is board vice president of Newhouse Sober Living in Santa Barbara, as well as president of the city's Alano Club for those in recovery. He is also certified in Smart Recovery, a non-profit recovery program.

David is a state-licensed real estate broker, former owner of two day spas, and once co-owned a vegan hair care line inspired by his daughter, Maya. A rock music aficionado since childhood, he still plays guitar in classic rock and roll bands.

In his three-plus decades of sobriety, David has helped tens of thousands of alcoholics and addicts in theirs. A featured speaker at 12-Step conventions, David has also carried the message to alcoholics and addicts at hospitals and institutions, as his first sponsors carried it to him, including giving the commencement address to graduates of the Lompoc, California federal facility's treatment program. He has blogged excerpts from his book at the popular sobriety website www.thefix.com.

David lives in Santa Barbara with his daughter.

CPSIA information can be obtained
at www.ICGtesting.com
Printed in the USA
FSHW012350150420
69235FS

9 781927 664155